HE SPEAKS, I LISTEN

Michelle McKinney Hammond

D0684382

HARVEST HOUSE PUBLISHERS
EUGENE, OREGON

Cover by Connie Gabbert Design + Illustration, Bend, OR

HE SPEAKS, I LISTEN
Taken from *His Love Always Finds Me*
Copyright © 1999 Michelle McKinney Hammond
Published by Harvest House Publishers
Eugene, Oregon 97402
www.harvesthousepublishers.com

ISBN 978-0-7369-6489-0 (pbk.)
ISBN 978-0-7369-6490-6 (eBook)

Printed in the United States of America

17 18 19 20 21 22 23 24 25 / BP-SK / 10 9 8 7 6 5 4 3 2 1

This one is for You, Lord.
Your love has sought me,
found me, bought me, and
kept me in Your light.
You are forever my Father,
always my Friend,
eternally the Lover of my soul.

In loving memory of my grandmother
Sarah Ayodele Sam.
She walked with God and was not,
for God took her,
but not before she showed me Jesus.

CONTENTS

IN THE HEART OF THE INNER JOURNEY

In the alone place
fear closes in
as I sense my aloneness
the part of me without You
that is lost
wandering in its own apprehensions
causing my spirit
to imitate a mime
pressing against invisible walls
that soundlessly threaten
suffocation by unconscious
yet deliberate isolation
And I long for the resuscitation
that Your breath brings
giving life to all my members
Strength to my soul
Causing me to unfold
like a wet new butterfly
fighting to unwrap itself
from the bondage of its
self-imposed cocoon
To spread new and unfamiliar members
for the very first time
testing their strength
readying these fragile members
for the act of ascending
Not caring for the fact
that it is the struggle
which produces strength
to take wing and fly

while resisting the urge
to cast off my independence
and call upon Your help
I weary myself
and wonder at my ability
to continue on
to rise above
where I presently lie...
This place is not kind
to my spirit's expectations
and I am lost in the prison of myself
while You patiently hold the key and wait...
wait for me to invite You into this alone place....

IN SOLITUDE

THE SWEET TIMES

*And the Lord God took the man, and put him into
the Garden of Eden to dress it and to keep it.*

GENESIS 2:15 KJV

Adam experienced something that no other man or woman (not even Eve) on the face of the earth has ever experienced. He had the incredible privilege of having God all to himself. In the beginning it was just him and God. Though Jesus and the Holy Ghost were present, the mystery of their Oneness was very evident. Every evening they had a date, and Adam had God's full attention. No interruptions in the prayer line. No one with a more urgent request. Just Adam and God.

Can you imagine such a sublime existence? To rise each morning and watch the sun stretch its arms across the sky in praise to God on High…to watch the flowers awaken, tilting their faces in serene worship toward their Creator while the rivers that run through the garden play a symphony of exuberant celebration against the banks of the shore and the birds sing their accompaniment, welcoming the morning and thanking God for another glorious day…. No telephone ringing, no alarm going off, no social media notifications, just the gentle breeze ever so gently rousing you, stirring your lashes, tickling your nose, almost kissing you, beckoning you to arise…. This was Adam's world. He rose to walk on a dew-covered carpet of grass, its pungent freshness filling the air with each step. Joyfully going about his tasks, anticipating his favorite time of the day….

And just about the time Adam thought he would burst with

expectation, it happened. The atmosphere in the garden changed. The animals stood still, ears tuned to something that no one saw. The birds stopped singing, waiting for a sound that was sweeter than their own. Even the wind seemed to hold its breath. And the sun came down for a closer look, leaving golden streaks across the sky to mark its place. Then the air was filled with the incense of the Lord's presence! The Lord God Himself had descended to the garden to walk and talk, face-to-face, with Adam. Nothing stood between them, for Adam was naked and unashamed. Perfect and good in every way. An extension of his Abba Father. A mirror reflection of the Trinity, spirit, soul, and body, unstained by sin.

It was…indescribable glory, this time of sweet communing. Every living thing in the garden seemed to be in a suspended state of reverent awe, clinging to God's every word. His still, small voice was like music. It was like the sound of falling rain, the sound of many waters, the ebbing of the tide. It rose and fell as He shared all that He was with Adam. God's words ignited Adam's soul and brought waves of refreshment to his spirit while Adam's worship of Him brought pleasure to His heart. It was a time of intimate fellowship…of deep communion…of unspeakable expressions and wordless impartations between man and his God. And then God withdrew with the promise of returning, His presence still lingering in the air like heady perfume.

Ah, to find our way back to the garden…This is the place in the cool of the evening of our lives when we finally grow still, finding our way back home. Back into the presence of God. Able once again to be open, vulnerable, honest, and uninhibited in the arms of the One who loves us most. To shut out the sound of every other voice and just listen, drinking in His Spirit. It is here that the world and all of its pressures and struggles become mere shadows that fade away as His comfort surrounds us. This is where we find peace, where we find refreshment. More importantly, this is where we find the center of our own being. This is where we find the strength to begin again.

Heavenly Father, help me to find my way back to our place of intimacy. It seems I don't visit this place enough. And yet when I finally meet You here, I wonder why it took me so long. Holy Spirit, call me and draw me to this place until my flesh rejoices to yield and enter into this sweet sanctuary of fellowship with You that my soul treasures. O Lord, help me to be as consistent in seeking You as You are in seeking me. Help me to keep ever fresh in my mind the joy of our last meeting, and never to lose the longing for more of You. In Jesus' name, amen.

When was the last time you spent quality time alone with God having a real heart-to-heart exchange with Him? What would you like to share with Him now?

_____

_____

_____

_____

_____

THE COMMUNING TIMES

And Enoch walked with God:
and he was not; for God took him.

GENESIS 5:24 KJV

He's out again, is he?" the visitor asked. Enoch's wife nodded her head in reply as she stirred the evening meal over the fire. "Where is it exactly that he goes?" questioned his friend, brows drawn together in perplexed punctuation. This was the third time he had tried to visit Enoch this week, only to find that he was nowhere to be found. "Wherever their conversation takes him," Enoch's wife serenely answered. She had grown used to these times. They did not frighten or disturb her. She only had to look into Enoch's eyes when he returned to know where he had been. Sometimes he was gone for an hour. Sometimes for days. And when he returned, his body weary but his eyes gleaming with a brilliant fire that burned from within, she knew he had been with God.

What they discussed she could only imagine. She herself tried to understand how it was possible for man and God to commune on such an intimate level. She tried to worship Him in the best way she knew, but she really couldn't say that God had ever spoken back. Enoch said it was because she didn't truly listen. She tried to listen, yet she heard nothing. She had grown beyond being jealous of her husband's deep, personal exchanges with God, choosing instead to let him share with her parts of their conversations. And, oh! What incredible things they were! Stories of what was to come. At first Enoch would eagerly tell these things to anyone who would listen. But many of these revelations were too deep, too awesome to be understood by those simply trying to keep up with their daily agenda of eking out a living for themselves. So more and more Enoch withdrew to his walks with God. He still returned with that same intense light burning in his eyes, but these days he also seemed increasingly pensive, as if his spirit were deeply pondering something profound and unspeakable. This she could respect.

Amazingly, no one ridiculed Enoch. Rather, they respectfully conceded that he truly was a man who sought God diligently. All who knew him admired this, and even promised themselves that they, too, would draw closer to God as soon as they got a little extra time on their hands. It was obvious that Enoch pleased God; he was blessed above and beyond measure. No one in their right mind would ever guess that he was three hundred and sixty-five years old. Why, he didn't look a day over one hundred and he was still having children! It was as if Enoch's conversations with God renewed his strength like the eagles'. He was always so full of energy. But what could they possibly find to talk about for hours—sometimes days—on end? Though many speculated, no one volunteered to accompany Enoch as he set off to fellowship with the Lord. It would have been almost impolite to do so, a most unwelcome intrusion. Yet countless eyes followed Enoch as he walked to his place of solitude to be with…Him.…

And so his wife prepared dinner and waited for his return. Once again she meditated upon how different her husband seemed these days after his time alone with God. More contemplative, lost in all he had been told. In the past he would return more vocal, warning his neighbors of God's judgment against those who were godless. But these days Enoch was silent, as if waiting for something to happen.

Slowly the night settled down around her. The embers of the

dinner fire had died, and still she waited for his return. The air around her held a tension she did not recognize, and she wondered what was different about this night. Then a voice, or perhaps it was just a quiet understanding, rose from within her spirit. "He won't be back," it whispered softly. She contemplated these words, quietly releasing her beloved husband into the hands of his Lord as she fell into a peaceful sleep.

And now here was his friend again, inquiring when Enoch would return. Why couldn't he understand what she so clearly knew? Enoch would not be back, for God had taken him. Yet this friend still insisted on searching for him. And everyone wondered at her serenity in the face of such deeply disturbing circumstances. "Poor dear," they all thought as they saw her set out, beginning the familiar pattern of her late husband. "Perhaps she will find him in one of her walks." Little did they know, it was not Enoch for whom she was seeking.

Enoch, the seventh generation born from Adam, was the foreshadow of yet another man who would literally be translated into the heavenly realm while still wrapped in living mortal flesh. Enoch had an extraordinary relationship with God, a deep intimacy, and a reputation that brought pleasure to the heart of the Father. For this he was rewarded by escaping the sting of death. Though this is the type of relationship with God we have the best of intentions to achieve, so many things distract us away from pressing into that place with Him.

How many times do we promise to spend more time communing with our Father? How many times do we come into His presence so laden down with our own cares that we hurriedly dump them at His feet, then dash away to extinguish yet another fire in our lives? And then we hear someone repeat something that God told them and we listen in envy, wondering, *Why doesn't God tell me things like that? Why doesn't He tell me anything, period?* With chagrin, we realize that we've been far too busy talking at God to listen to Him. And yet the only way to be translated to a place far above our circumstances is to immerse ourselves in Him.

> *Dear Heavenly Father, please forgive me for my misplaced priorities. Forgive me for answering the call of the world instead of stealing away with You. Although I know I was created for Your good pleasure, I spend far too much time seeking pleasures of my own. As You await me becoming a true worshiper who will worship You in spirit and in truth, I fill my world with helpless idols and seek more blatant answers that won't require any surrender or transparency on my part. And though I long to please You, I fear what I will become if I do all that You require. Help me to forsake all but Your heart and find my pleasure in pleasing You. Help me to realize that my greatest reward at the end of the day is You and the power You possess to translate me above all that binds me. In Jesus' name, amen.*

What have you allowed to stand in the way of your quiet time with God? What things do you need to reprioritize in your life to get back to the place of regular fellowship with Him? What would you like to have happen in your relationship with Him? What are you willing to do in order to make that happen? Write a commitment of renewal to the Lord that you can place on your heart and run with.

_____

_____

_____

_____

_____

THE BINDING TIMES

*When the sun went down, and it was dark, behold
a smoking furnace, and a burning lamp that
passed between those pieces. In the same day
the LORD made a covenant with Abram.*

GENESIS 15:17-18 KJV

Abram didn't know if it was the night air or beholding this sight, both awesome and terrible, that caused him to be chilled to the bone. He felt every hair on his body stand on end as the presence of God saturated his understanding with visions of things that God would not speak. However, His demonstration spoke loud and clear. Abram had pondered the Lord's words all afternoon as he gathered together a heifer, a goat, a ram, a dove, and a young pigeon. "I will be your great reward..." The words echoed in his spirit as he cut each animal in two, with the exception of the birds, and arranged the halves opposite each other in obedience to God. "I will be your great reward..." *What could that possibly mean?* thought Abram. *How could God being my reward solve my immediate problems?*

He felt an ache every time he saw the look on his wife's face as she gazed at a mother holding her child. And he felt helpless. Helpless to give Sarai the one thing she truly wanted—a son. Truly, God had richly blessed them with everything else. But this one thing. This one thing was like a wet blanket snuffing out the joy of everything else. How could God being his reward resolve this conflict between joy and pain, comfort and longing? Yet Abram willingly obeyed his Lord, preparing the animals He requested, and he waited. For the Lord had promised him descendants as numerous as the stars, and Abram believed Him. God had called him out and away from all that he was accustomed to with the promise of possessing a new land, and He had proven Himself along the way, increasing Abram's wealth in measures untold. Yet this one thing was different from any other area of his life. His other prayers had been answered almost instantly, but this one thing lingered. It became a greater question day by day. As time became a foe against his desire, his need for a greater assurance from God became increasingly pressing.

And now God had given him a sign. An awesome sign, sealing his promise to Abram that his descendants, birthed from his own seed, would be more numerous than the stars. More numerous than his ability to count. And greater still, his descendants would possess this new land that God had brought him to! This was more than he had dared hope for, yet he believed God's promise. But still this nagging need for affirmation burned within his heart. And now here in this place of meeting, as the sun sought solace from the heat of the day on the backside of the hills, Abram fought the exhaustion of his efforts to wait on God. To hear a clear word. To receive some sign, some indication that God would keep this promise he was almost afraid to cling to. Then God's whisper interrupted the dusk, answering Abram's questions with dreadful revelations as He unfolded the fate of Abram's lineage yet to come. The darkness of separation that his people would feel as they experienced the bonds of slavery in Egypt before returning to this land. Abram could not imagine this. As long as he had known God, he had known liberty and wealth.

Abram recalled the day he first heard God's voice telling him to forsake everything he held dear and follow Him away from his family and his country to a new land that He would show him. Something told him he could trust this voice, and he followed willingly. Still, their relationship had never been tested in this way. Feeling the need for more visible support, he took his nephew Lot with him. Abram soon found out why the Lord had suggested that he go alone. God had known all along that those outside of the vision He gives become a time-consuming distraction from the true blessing that awaits. In time, Abram learned he had no need for Lot or to cling to familiar crutches, so the two men parted company. Abram came to trust God as a constant in his life; truly, He was the "friend that sticketh closer than a brother" (Proverbs 18:24 KJV).

So here Abram was—where God had wanted him to be in the first place—alone with Him. In His presence nothing overshadowed Him, not even the sun. And so in the darkness of its absence, God became Abram's only light. As the blood flowed between the carcasses, it was joined by a smoking firepot and a flaming torch, sealing the matter between this man and his God. Yes, God would keep His word. Even this one thing was not too difficult for Him to accomplish. With this knowledge, God sealed His promise to Abram by literally putting His word on the line, making a binding covenant through the fire, the light, and the blood. And because He had no one greater to swear by, He swore by Himself to bring to pass what He had promised in His own irrevocable way.

When our desires surround our heart so tightly that we feel alone inside of our dreams, God is present lighting the way, holding a flaming torch aloft to guide our steps toward our destiny, making us worthy to receive the promise with the purifying fire of His own holiness and the cleansing flow of sacrificial blood.

> *Heavenly Father, You have blessed me in so many ways that I almost feel ashamed to ask You for one more thing. And yet my heart is overwhelmed with longing and my desire weighs heavily upon my soul. I feel as if You've said yes, but the promise seems to take so long to become a manifested reality. I wonder if Your promise is simply my imagination and my own flesh willing You to be in agreement with me. As I lay my longing at Your feet once more, please speak a sure word to my spirit. Grant me Your assurance that You will come bearing the answer and lighting the way to my heart's treasure. In Jesus' name, amen.*

What is the desire that you feel isolated in harboring? God has a covenant promise for you. Won't you write the vision and make it plain so you can run with His promise sealed upon your heart?

Write the reasons for your doubts. Then give them to God once and for all.

THE AWESOME TIMES

When Jacob awoke from his sleep, he thought, "Surely the Lord is in the place, and I was not aware of it." He was afraid and said, "How awesome is this place! This is none other than the house of God; this is the gate of heaven."

GENESIS 28:16-17

Still wiping the sleep from his eyes, Jacob tried to separate reality from his dreams but found the two immutably bound. There was no separating them. The stairway from heaven to earth was real. The angels ascending and descending were no hazy vision. The angel of the Lord was no apparition, for his promise rang true. He had indeed been visited by God in this place. There was no one to deny or confirm what was happening here, just his own soul bearing witness to this incredible happening. But what his comprehension could not grasp was why? Why would God promise him anything? Especially after what he had done. Didn't God know what everybody else knew—that Jacob was here in the wilderness because of his own underhandedness? Why did this God, who insisted on holiness according to his father, feel he was worthy to receive such a promise?

The blessing he had deceitfully taken from his father's hands and stolen from his brother's legacy God now freely gave without any tricks on his part. Jacob didn't know how to respond. He was used to tit for tat. Some sort of bargain had to be struck. After all, no one ever got anything for free. So Jacob decided to forge his own deal with God, on his own terms, in order to solidify their understanding. If God would be with him, provide for him, and bring him back to this place, *then* he, Jacob, would give God permission to be his God. And God silently agreed, watched Jacob go his own way, and waited for him to discover that the only One who truly kept His promises was God Himself. But they were ultimately made on His terms.

So Jacob bargained with Laban for the hand of Rachel and found himself betrayed. The trickster had finally met his match. Only the mercy of God could give him the upper hand. God gracefully kept His promise, preserving him even in the face of Laban's cleverness until it was clearly apparent to Jacob what must become obvious to us all—that "but for the grace of God go I." Yet God had more to teach him.

After years of struggling to live one step ahead of his father-in-law's manipulations, Jacob finally headed home. Surrounded by all of his possessions, his household, his children, and his wives, he felt rather fortified until he received news that his brother Esau was on his way to meet him. With this news, the old Jacob returned. Trusting the Lord was out, and leaning to his own understanding was in big time.

After sending his entourage and family ahead to guard them from any attack that might occur, Jacob found himself in the very place he had been avoiding. Forsaken by his own wiles and schemes, he was now forced to depend totally on God at the most threatening point in his life. This was a completely new experience for Jacob, and he wrestled with it. *How do I get rid of myself?* he wondered. *How do I get to the place of "No longer I, but God in me," when "me" is all I've relied on for as long as I can remember?* Jacob was frightened. He was letting go to release himself into God-only-knows what instead of holding on to *something*, even if it was "puttin' a hurtin'" on him, as the old folks say. And so the angel of the Lord allowed Jacob to wrestle with him until the break of day. To the breaking point. For it is only at the breaking point that we begin to see the light.

And still Jacob clung, afraid to let go without an assurance, a blessing, from God. Jacob was still clinging to what Jacob knew. But no blessing came until Jacob admitted who he was—which was *where* he was. And then the grace of God released him to be a new man. A man outside of himself. Whole and free. Naked and wounded by the knowledge that he had gained nothing in his own strength but that which God had allowed. How much easier life would have been if Jacob had simply yielded to the hand of the One who freely gives! But the greater tragedy would have been if he'd never arrived at this point of understanding.

In this "you've got to make it happen" world, we've gotten snowed into thinking we have to "help God" in order to obtain what we think we want or need. And we, like Jacob, often find ourselves forsaken by our own machinations. Suffering from the backlash of what we considered a successful manipulation, we attempt to strike another bargain, then find ourselves in even deeper trouble. Flailing, wrestling, unwilling to let go of the old way of doing things, we hang on for dear life, determined to make it work. And God quietly says, "Let go," to which we reply, "No! Not until You show me what I'm going to get out of this!" He fails to answer, but instead poses another question: "Who do you think you are?" But the real questions are, "Who are you, really? And how much further do you think you can get without My assistance?" And we are forced to grudgingly admit our finiteness and deposit our limping egos into the arms of God, who blesses us in spite of ourselves.

Dear Heavenly Father, I admit my own weakness. I admit my own attempts to assist You in blessing me have failed miserably. I even admit that my own selfishness has caused me to grasp at my own desires with no thought of those around me. So I deposit all that I've gained for myself back at Your feet. All of my fleshly manipulations, plots, and schemes. I lay them beside my dreams and offer them back to You. I know that in Your fairness, You will bless me without costing others. Please forgive me for my lack of trusting Your heart toward me. Help me to rest more securely in Your love and Your desire to bless me above measure. Help me not to be moved by what my eyes see, but only what my heart hears from You. In Jesus' name, amen.

What things in your life have you felt the necessity to take care of yourself? In what areas do you doubt God's lack of interest or best of intentions toward you? What have you been afraid to release into His care? Make a list and sacrifice these things back to the Lord right now.

_____

_____

_____

_____

_____

There You are!
I thought I had lost You
but instead I have found You
where You've always been
Still my Father
Still my Friend
Still my source of Consolation
Soothing all the places
that were ravaged from
strangers who caught me
wandering down my own path
seeking my own way
which always leads me
back to You
back to who I truly am....

THE REVEALING TIMES

Now Moses was tending the flock of Jethro his father-in-law, the priest of Midian, and he led the flock to the far side of the wilderness and came to Horeb, the mountain of God. There the angel of the LORD appeared to him in flames of fire from within a bush.

EXODUS 3:1-2

Moses stooped to remove his sandals with trembling fingers, wondering to himself at the strange sight he beheld. Not knowing whether to hide his face or to sneak another look, he cowered in awe at this apparition...*or was it?* He couldn't tell. But then again, this...phenomenon (yes, that was a better word for it) had a voice. This vision claimed to be God and, more incredibly, said He wanted to use him, Moses, to deliver the Israelites out of the bondage they suffered in Egypt! Didn't He know that Moses was a man on the run? Didn't He know of his crime? Didn't He know he couldn't talk properly? If He were truly God, then surely He would know that Moses was hardly qualified for such a lofty mission!

Yes, he had been raised in Pharaoh's house. Yes, he knew the ins and outs of the court. Yes, he had been trained in all manner of Egyptian knowledge and etiquette. BUT...and this was a very big but...everyone knew by now that Moses was a Hebrew with no power himself, reduced to living as a fugitive. It seemed that he was always out of place, a fish out of water, isolated from those around him because he was different. From the day his mother placed him in a hand-woven basket and sailed him down the Nile in order to save his life he became a stranger among the familiar. Rescued and raised by Pharaoh's daughter, the tug to be grateful and enjoy an enviable fate was juxtaposed with championing the cause of his people who did not share as posh a life as he. He was caught between two cultures, considered an outsider to both. To the Egyptians he was a Hebrew, a mere charity case they indulged for the sake of Pharaoh's daughter who sheltered him under her care. To the Hebrews he was a wannabe who had denied his roots to live in Pharaoh's house. Even the relationship between his brother, Aaron, his sister, Miriam, and himself, though loving, seemed strained. And who could blame them? They lived worlds apart even though in close proximity, their experiences totally foreign to one another.

And now after killing a cruel Egyptian overseer, he had fled to Midian to escape the wrath of Pharaoh. What could God be thinking? How could He send him back to Egypt? What welcome would he find there after all this time? Who could he truly call family? What lineage could he point to in order to validate himself in the eyes of those he was called to lead? Who would be on his side? Yet God said He would be with him. But who was this God? What were His credentials? Who would Moses say had sent him? And then came the words that made Moses' heart explode… "I Am That I Am."

"I Am That I Am…" "I Am That I Am!" Within those words were a million answers! I Am He who gives sight to the blind, speech to the mute, strength to the weak, faith to the helpless, provision to those who lack, security to the wandering, a deliverer to the bound…whatever it is that you need, I Am that! And right now Moses needed a lot. He needed courage. He needed affirmation. Affirmation that he belonged. Belonged to someone, that his roots were secure, that there was someone in his life that truly had his back. And here was God saying He was all that Moses was searching for.

But just in case that wasn't enough for Moses, He would allow his brother, Aaron, to assist him in this important assignment although this was not His preference. And so, with the assistance of Aaron's eloquent speech and God's miracles to back him up, Moses found security in his calling and led the people of Israel out. But even this great success was not enough to make his heart at home among his people. He still felt the gulf between them. They were hesitant to approach God for themselves, yet were antagonistic toward what they termed his position of favor with God. After all, who was he to tell them what to do? Just because he got to see God face-to-face, why should he lord it over them? Poor Moses couldn't win for losing. The more he tried to accommodate their insecurities in order to be accepted, the more they misinterpreted his benevolence for spiritual pride. In the end when God's wrath burned against the people, the same ones he defended cost him his dream—to enter the Promise Land. Yes, Moses learned the hard way that in the face of "Who do you think you are?" there can only be one answer: Because He Is, I am. No apologies.

"Who am I?" many of us ask. In search of our identity it is important to know that it really doesn't matter who we are as long as He Is. In Him our identity is made secure. The search ends before His throne. Once yielded to His Spirit He illuminates our understanding and unfolds the mystery of who we really are and who He has created us to be. This is privileged information for us and us alone. If no one else gets it, that's all right because it doesn't change God's design. So let them murmur and know when to let go of the stragglers, releasing yourself back into the arms of the One who knows you best.

> *Dear Heavenly Father, I am so guilty of trying to win*
> *everyone's approval except Yours and it always costs me*
> *a piece of myself. Why the search for outward validation*
> *consumes me I will never know, but You do. You see to*
> *the core of my soul. I ask that You would make me secure*
> *in You. That the search for who I really am would end*
> *before Your presence. Fill me with Yourself and who*
> *You are. Let me rejoice in my new identity as You write*
> *Your name upon my heart. You are my Abba Father*
> *and in that I can rest. And when I've come to the end*
> *of myself and I question my own identity, lead me back*
> *to the truth that in You I am. In Jesus' name, amen.*

What areas of self-doubt do you struggle with? Write a faith confession of who you are in Christ that you can rehearse to build up your inner person. Choose a scripture to memorize that would be useful when you feel overwhelmed by feelings of insecurity and insignificance.

THE CHALLENGING TIMES

*When the angel of the LORD appeared to Gideon,
he said, "The LORD is with you, mighty warrior."
"Pardon me, my lord," Gideon replied, "but if the
LORD is with us, why has all this happened to us?"*

JUDGES 6:12

Glancing furtively over his shoulder to make sure no one was watching, Gideon tossed the wheat into the air and watched the kernels lift and separate from the chaff as the wind interrupted their upward ascent. He thought back to the days when he enjoyed the kiss of the sun on his shoulders and the exhilaration of the breeze sweeping across his face as he threshed his harvest atop a hill. It was such a liberating feeling to be out in the open air, watching the wheat sparkle as it twirled upward. It was amazing how it took no more than a gust of wind to divide the empty from that which was essential. Gideon pondered this often as he repeated the process year after year. But now those times of enjoyment were over. They had been over for seven years. He had been reduced to doing this task secretly in a winepress, away from the eyes of those who were his people's enemies—the Midianites.

For far too long the countryside had groaned under the terrorism and destruction of this band of nomads who timed their visitations with the harvest. For seven years the Israelites planted their crops. And for seven years the Midianites, Amalekites, and other eastern peoples invaded the country, destroying all that they planted and killing all their herds until they were reduced to being fugitives in their own land—preparing shelters for themselves in mountain clefts, caves, and strongholds; trying to salvage what they could under cover; wondering aloud if God would ever deliver them.

And now sensing an unknown presence in his private sanctuary, Gideon, fearing discovery by an enemy, whirled around to face a stranger who seemed to appear out of nowhere and greet him with even stranger words. Him, a warrior? He in no way felt like a warrior. Try victim. Try defeated. But hardly would a warrior be found skulking around in this manner, barely eking out an existence. And if God was with him, He sure had a funny way of showing it. As for being the chosen vessel to save his people out of the hand of the Midianites, that was truly a laugh! He was the least in his family, his clan was the weakest in Manasseh. Was this some sort of cruel joke? Yet something inside of him dared to hope, dared to make a sacrifice, dared to listen to what this bearer of these unbelievable tidings had to say.

As the offering was consumed, Gideon's faith was ignited. A boldness that was willing to shatter the altars of compromise his people had built rose up within him. Yet not inclined to face the wrath of his family and the men of the town, he chose the shelter of night along with ten of his servants to annihilate his father's altar to Baal and the Asherah pole beside it. His spirit felt the same exhilaration he felt on the hilltops while threshing as he burnt a sacrifice to the Lord with the wood that had once been a memorial to a foreign god. Truly, the wheat was now being separated from the chaff.

Just as Gideon suspected would be the case, the town's cries of indignation rose with the morning sun in a loud, discordant chorus. Perhaps his father, Joash, surveying the remains of the sacrifice, was jolted into remembering the former days when the Lord God had shown Himself mighty on their behalf. For now he steadfastly defended his son, declaring that if Baal were truly the god they thought he was, then he should rise to his own defense. Feeling totally affirmed by his father and girded up by the Spirit of the Lord coming upon him, Gideon sounded the trumpet to arms against their enemies, no longer feeling alone. And God, not willing to share His glory with a large company of men, did a final threshing and separating before allowing Gideon and his elite army to proceed onward to victory. God showed Himself to be ever present in Gideon's life, and Gideon became a mighty man of valor, no longer fearful of stepping out against those who challenged him.

How often do we wonder where God is in the midst of situations that repeatedly beat us down time and time again? Our faith often becomes lost in the shuffle of dire circumstances that life continually deals us. We stumble into compromising our standards in order to survive, tripping over the enemy's lies that we are insignificant, disowned, unloved, and defenseless. But then the Lord Himself goes before us and clears the way, reminding us that if we don't walk in total trust and obedience before Him, victory will remain elusive.

Dear Heavenly Father, forgive me for the many times
I walked away from You devising my own way, then
turned back again to question Your lack of faithfulness.
Forgive me for the idols I have built that block my vision
of You standing there waiting to assist me out of my
troubles. Please help me to tear down the idols in my

life and call on You and You alone. Help me to resist the
urge to compromise my standards because of my lack
of trust in You. Help me to internalize Your promises
and stand on them with unwavering allegiance. Help
me to separate the lies of the enemy from Your truth.
Liberate me to rest in Your strength, knowing that You
are my defense and my deliverer. In Jesus' name, amen.

When the enemy is clearly present and God seems increasingly absent, what altars do you build in your life to secure the things that are important to you? What do you need to clear away in order for God to have room to move on your behalf? Make a list and offer it as a sacrifice to Him right now.

THE BROKEN TIMES

He awoke from his sleep and thought, "I'll go
out as before and shake myself free." But he
did not know that the LORD had left him.

JUDGES 16:20

Samson squirmed to find a more comfortable position on the dank floor of the prison. The bronze shackles that bound his ankles chafed against his skin and left their mildewed marks like green tattoos. He smoothed the fresh new locks of hair back from his forehead, thinking how ironic it was that the thing that had gotten him into the most trouble was gone too late —his eyes. His eyes had always gotten him in trouble. For instance, he wished he had never laid eyes on Delilah. And now what he could no longer see haunted him night after night in dreams that turned quickly to nightmares filled with a million screaming regrets. How could he have been such a fool? Philistine women couldn't be trusted. Why hadn't he learned his lesson with the Philistine girl he had married? His parents had tried to tell him, but no, he wouldn't listen. After all, he was invincible. Who could hurt him? Samson learned too late that he was his most injurious enemy.

Delilah had been so beautiful, so compliant to all his fleshly wishes. She wasn't like the women from among his people, always frowning and reminding him of his calling when he wanted to indulge in a little sport. Delilah didn't care that he was a Nazarite priest; she just wanted to please him. And he just wanted to be pleased. After all, being a judge over Israel was hard work. Settling disputes, leading fights against their enemies…at the end of the day he deserved a little levity, a little harmless amusement in the form of a good woman who wasn't religious or demanding. But now all that he had loved about Delilah made Samson sick to his stomach as he saw through the whole trap.

How could he have believed that she loved him? He had been so flattered when she wondered at his extraordinary strength. He had so enjoyed showing off for her, escaping the grip of the Philistines who were constantly trying to entrap him. He had teased her, making up amusing stories about the source of his strength when she asked. But her questions had become more and more insistent. She complained that he didn't really love her at all if he chose not to confide in her. And still he never thought back to when another Philistine woman who had betrayed him, his wife, had done the same. No, Samson was too caught up in the haze of her perfume and that incredible incense she burned in the room whenever he was there. His defenses were lowered by the wine she served. Of course he loved her, he argued. Could he please just get a bit of sleep, a tender kiss, a little peace? But she hounded him and hounded him until he saw no rest in sight and finally came clean with her. And she responded by dealing him the dirty hand of betrayal. Luring him to sleep in her lap, she held him in deceitful arms while her partner in crime shaved off the seven braids that held the secret of Samson's strength.

He awoke to find himself surrounded by the Philistines but forsaken by those he had counted on—Delilah, God, his own strength…gone. Those who had previously quaked in fear before him now gouged out his eyes, mercilessly dragging him away to be treated like a common slave grinding grain in a prison. Sad to say, Samson now saw clearly what he had never seen before—his own foolishness. His utter disregard for sound counsel. His disrespect of God and His calling. The needs of the people that God had entrusted into his care. All of this had escaped his vision as he focused on his own personal pursuits.

He was almost too embarrassed to ask for God's assistance now. But for as much as he had been self-indulgent, he needed to give serving God one last-ditch effort. At this point, the only redeemable effort would be to annihilate as many of the Hebrews' enemies as he could in one fatal swoop. For this he would need God's help. Finally Samson understood that he could not do this in his own strength. With this resolved, he entered the arena where the Philistines had all gathered to pay homage to their god, Dagon. And Samson asked God to be his companion once more. The body that he refused to present as a living sacrifice, to prove what had been God's good, acceptable, and perfect will concerning his life, he now realized had been his reasonable service in exchange for all that God had given him. As the pillars of the temple began to topple beneath his touch, that which he withheld before he now gladly offered. And he surmised in his final thoughts that a moment of honor birthed through the labor of obedience was far sweeter than a life filled with meaningless seductions.

Sometimes the mistakes we've made seem unredeemable. We find ourselves bowed over in bondage to the pain of the consequences that rebellion brings. Self-debasement and condemnation make the load more than we can bear as we cringe in the mirror of our own foolishness. But God's grace meets us even in this place. And as we own up to our sin, recognizing what we refused to see before, so blinded were we with the immediate cravings of our own desires, He sends His own strength to refresh us, renew us, and help us stand again.

> *Dear Heavenly Father, so many times I allow the lust of my eyes to override the direction of Your Spirit. Please help me keep the bigger picture in view. Help me to have a greater passion for fulfilling my God-ordained destiny than fulfilling the immediate desires of the flesh. Even when I don't know all of the details, help my trust in You to be a bridge over the chasm of the questions my heart can't answer. Please meet me in my moments of failure, forgive and restore me, and give me the opportunity to triumph again. In Jesus' name, amen.*

Where do you feel you have failed others, yourself, and God lately? As you look at the rubble of bad decisions before you, begin to pile them up before His throne and allow Him to bring restoration to the broken places. Make a list of new resolutions to address your weaknesses. Find a scripture that you can memorize, confess, and apply to your situation. Write it down and chart a course for your new beginning.

THE COMMISSIONING TIMES

Then Eli realized that the Lord was calling the boy.
So Eli told Samuel, "Go and lie down, and if he calls
you, say, 'Speak, Lord, for you servant is listening.'"
So Samuel went and lay down in his place.

1 SAMUEL 3:8-9

Samuel lay in the dark, listening to the night sounds around him, reflecting on his mother's last visit to him. He really enjoyed his duties in the temple and Eli was just like a father to him, yet he looked forward to his mother, Hannah, coming every year bearing gifts and loads of love and comfort. These were special times in which she always reminded him of how she had prayed diligently for him and God had answered her prayer. In gratitude she had dedicated him back to the service of the Lord. "Samuel," she told him, "never forget that you are a special gift from God. You must always bring pleasure to His heart in return for His mercy and kindness." She warned him against behaving like Eli's sons who were fueling the gossip mill with their disgraceful behavior. All were horrified at their blatant disregard for the things of God. They didn't even try to hide how they skimmed off the best of the offerings that the people brought to the Lord. And the womanizing! Everyone knew Eli's sons were sleeping with the women who worked at the entrance to the Tent of Meeting. Eli had confronted them, but they had only scorned his rebuke and continued to anger God and man with their flagrant rebellion. Samuel had purposed he would never bring sorrow to his mother's heart as Eli's sons brought to their father's.

Samuel mulled upon all of these things as he stared into the darkness, waiting for sleep to come. He thought about the stories Eli told about how God used to speak to the people and give His prophets visions of things to come. Samuel had never experienced this, and he wondered what it would be like to actually hear the voice of God. What exactly would His voice sound like? Would it be frightening or contain some distinct quality that set it apart from human voices? He would like to experience hearing God's voice one day… Just as he was drifting off to sleep, he heard a voice calling softly from the edge of his consciousness, "Samuel…Samuel…" "Yes, here I am," he replied. *Perhaps Eli is thirsty and needs a drink,* he thought, getting up and walking to Eli's room. It was difficult for the old man to find his way around at night now that his sight was growing dimmer and dimmer. But much to Samuel's confusion, his hasty appearance in Eli's room jolted his mentor out of a sound sleep. *Hmm, that's strange,* he thought as he returned to his own room. *Perhaps Eli didn't know he had called out in his sleep…Wait! There it is again.* By the third reoccurrence, Samuel stood looking befuddled at the irritated Eli, who had been roused thrice and looked none too pleased at these constant interruptions.

But slowly something dawned on Eli. This was not simply the boy's imagination. Samuel was indeed being summoned…by the Lord! His heart leapt within him. Perhaps God was once again ready to manifest Himself as He had in days gone by! And so, with Eli's gentle instruction ringing in his ears, Samuel returned to his pallet and waited to see if the Lord would call him again. It seemed as if an eternity passed but it was just a few moments before the Lord—this time he knew—came and stood before Samuel and called to him. Once. Twice. Finally Samuel found his tongue and repeated what Eli had told him to say: "Speak, for Your servant is listening."

Along with the recognition of the Lord's voice came revelations, some of which Samuel was disinclined to repeat. And so he pondered this strange new experience until morning. Lost in thought as he automatically went through his daily ritual, he was jolted from his reverie by Eli calling him; Samuel could now recognize the difference between the two voices. Reluctantly he answered, for he knew that Eli would want to know what God had said. And Samuel was unwilling to be the bearer of bad news to one who had been so kind to him. At this moment he felt isolated by the information he hid in his bosom, fearing Eli's response to the news that God was displeased with his family and that punishment would soon visit his house. Would he accuse Samuel of being a presumptuous upstart whose ego had been inflated overnight because of God's one conversation with him? And what of Eli's sons, who treated him with veiled disdain because he was so "holy" already? What if Eli told his sons that Samuel had prophesied that God was going to judge them? What cruel retaliation would they plan for him?

But Eli yielded to even this harsh news from the Lord, and Samuel was encouraged never to hide what God had disclosed to him. And God, seeing that he could trust Samuel to repeat what He relayed, continued to reveal Himself to him through His word. Samuel's boldness never failed through appointing, then impeaching Saul, and appointing David as king over Israel. No one stood against him, for all knew that Samuel was proven as a prophet of the Lord. Truly, friendship with God was to be trusted more than the shifting approval of men.

This is the type of fellowship we long for with God. But then

He comes, bearing news that isn't exactly what we had anticipated, calling us to action, making us responsible for what we've heard. *Is that truly You, Lord?* we are tempted to ask, at times not being able to discern His voice from our own opinions. Sometimes lifting the standard of God's Word in a place where it is seemingly disregarded can be most alienating. We wonder if we should say something or keep what we know to ourselves. But God stands waiting for the use of our voices; therefore, He truly stands beside us.

> *Dear Heavenly Father, I remember times when I failed to recognize Your voice. Times when the truth of Your Word was too much for me to bear. Please help me to have the courage to receive what You say and to follow You unwaveringly. Help me not to fear the faces of people when You call me to speak a word of truth, reproof, or correction to them. Still the quaking of my heart and fill me with boldness. Fill me with a passion for the truth that refuses to compromise in the face of opposition. Help me to remember that I represent You first and foremost, and that my obedience to You is essential to my wholeness and peace of mind and spirit. Keep me close to You. Let not even Your whisper be lost to my ears, oh, Lord. I long to hear all that You have to say and do Your bidding. In Jesus' name, amen.*

Can you recall the last thing the Lord shared with you, either through a spoken word, His written Word, or a word of encouragement from someone in your midst? Write it down here and treasure it. Find scriptures to confirm the word, and meditate on His promise to you with a heart of expectancy.

_____

_____

_____

_____

_____

As the deer pants for streams of water,
so my soul pants for you, O God.
My soul thirsts for God, for the living God.
Where can I go and meet with God?

PSALM 42:1-2

THE INTIMATE TIMES

I have seen you in the sanctuary and beheld your power
and your glory. Because your love is better than life,
my lips will glorify you. I will praise you as long as I live.

PSALM 63:2-4

avid's eyes scanned the expanse of the wilderness. It reflected the way his spirit felt. Dry. Empty. Parched. Longing for a drop of refreshment. A fresh wind of relief. The air was as still as his heart, hoping and praying for God to move, to speak, to do something, anything that would put a period on this portion of his life. Being back in this place brought back too many memories. Some were sweet and distant, some too fresh and painful to dwell on for any length of time. It was so ironic that he, a king, would be in his present position. A fugitive in his own domain. Running from his own son. It was easier to understand why he ran from Saul many years ago. After all, Saul had been an enemy, afraid of losing his kingdom. But his own son! This treachery David took personally. Yet it was times like this that were ideal for grounding, refocusing, reassessing where he had come from.

As David backtracked through the years in his mind, he thought of the times before his household had lurched out of control, fueled by lust and bitterness. He recalled the times before his son Amnon raped his stepsister Tamar, and their brother Absalom retaliated by having Amnon murdered. He remembered the days before his own scandalous affair with Bathsheba and his shameful hit on her husband, Uriah. Even before the times of dancing victoriously before the Lord after a hard-won battle there had been simpler times. Priceless times tucked away within a secret place inside him, times spent in green pastures. Times when the Lord and his father's flocks were his only companions. This was where David released his soul into the arms of God and found perfect rest. The presence of his Lord was evident in everything around him. From the coolness of the grass beneath his feet to the sweetness of the streams that calmly wound on their way to the protective trees shading him from the glare of the noonday sun. Truly, this was God's sitting room, and he, David, had been invited as a pampered guest.

And so he did the only thing he could think of to show his gratitude to his gracious host. David played Him songs of worship. He poured out his heart to the Lord, singing of His goodness and His glory. Songs of love and adoration filled the air. Even the birds stopped to listen and bow their heads in agreement. This was life at its best. What his other brothers deemed as tedious work and avoided, he gladly embraced, viewing the hours spent tending sheep as a precious rendezvous with God. Perhaps the Lord had indulged David because He knew of the times that were set before him—times when he would valiantly fight giants and foreigners alike for the freedom of his people. When he would be pursued for years and dodge death at the hands of a paranoid, schizophrenic king. When matters of state, palace intrigue, mounting family pressures, and people around him jostling for position would all overshadow those serene days when he had answered to only one voice...the voice of the Lord. David arched back his neck, welcoming the warm rays from above, and breathed out, "Thank God for those times!" They were a million miles removed from praying on the rooftop of the palace. How many times had he perused the countryside from his bedroom window, mulling on those moments of fellowship that now had to be snatched in bits and pieces from the day's demands?

It was not that God had moved away but rather that he, David, felt the distance widening as the pull of the world around him separated him from that former closeness. But now, as he stood looking at the direction from whence he had come, the palace now completely out of view, his heart rose up within him. *Thank You for the reminder, God, that though my present circumstance seems dire, yet will I praise You. I know who You are. I've seen You. I've heard You before. I know how sweet life can be with You and You alone. And when all is said and done, nothing compares to You. How I thirst for You! How I long to feel Your embrace in the wind. To feel Your touch in the sun. To see Your eyes twinkle in the starlight. This I've grown to appreciate because I've experienced it all, Lord. And nothing—not riches, not fame, not the most beautiful women or the most priceless possessions—compares to You. One moment with You is far sweeter than a lifetime of acquisitions.*

Do you remember when your relationship with the Lord was new? How you couldn't wait to steal away and spend time with Him? Every moment was richly treasured, and then the business of doing God's work took over. The passion that was once directed toward God became diverted to the tasks at hand. Things like this happen. We all make mistakes. We crash and burn. We find ourselves alone again, far from the fickle masses. And then we look upward with a new perspective, realizing that all the things we fight and scrape for are not important at all. And we remember that the most important thing in life is what it was from the beginning... our relationship with our Heavenly Father.

*Dear Heavenly Father, thank You for always offering
cooling streams when our hearts have grown parched
from the heat and pressure of all the external affairs
that surround us. Sometimes doing distracts us from
being who You made us to be—worshipers. Help me to
remember, above all things, that as I pursue You and
bring pleasure to Your heart, You will guard my affairs
and make even my enemies to be at peace with me. Help
me to remember that the true place of refreshment and
completion is before Your throne. During times when I
feel a hunger and a thirst that nothing else seems to fill,
help me to have the presence of mind to understand that
it is You who my soul really craves. Fill me and satisfy
me with Yourself once more. In Jesus' name, amen.*

What things have you allowed to distract you away from your First Love? Reflect back to a time when you overflowed with peace and joy, and rehearse the moments you spent with God then. Take inventory of what you need to do to get back on track—back into that sweet place with God again.

I have learned of
        another space called time
        that calls sweetly to me
            That woos me gently to its bosom
            causing me to rest in the discovery
                that it is in the alone times
                    that I find You
            refreshing me like newly falling dew
        Washing me in my own tears
    imparting Your comfort
            like liquid oil soothing my heart
            melting my defenses
            and all the reasons
                why I deny You
            until I find myself back in this place
                where fellowship is sweet communion
            where intimacy is second nature
    Where I am reminded of Your faithfulness
        and Your love for me…
    Yet there is a time called alone that I fear
        but cannot seem to flee
            for an invisible arm grips me suddenly
    unexpectedly
            while supports I counted true vanish
            daring me to keep my standards
                in the face of a million opposing voices
    I stand in the cold
        shivering from my own indecision
    torn by the reality
        of how little I trust You
            as my stomach knots in hunger
                for one word of reassurance
                    from You who holds the key to my wholeness
                    that I am really not alone…

THE WEARY TIMES

When he came to Beersheba in Judah, he left his
servant there, while he himself went a day's journey
into the wilderness. He came to a broom tree, sat
down under it and prayed that he might die.

1 KINGS 19:3-4

Elijah was tired. So tired that he was too tired to even vocalize the feeling. There were no words to express this degree of consuming exhaustion. *Where was his reward in serving God?* he wondered. Was this the thanks he got for standing up to the prophets of Baal? For making a mockery of their so-called god? He could still remember the absolute incredulity that came over their faces when God's fire fell and consumed the sacrifice he had prepared for Him. The fire had consumed everything—the sacrifice, the wood, the stones, the soil, even the water in the trench that had been dug around it. That was all the people needed to see to fall on their faces and worship God. Incensed against the prophets of Baal, the crowd rose and slaughtered them all. And then Elijah had prophesied an end to the drought in the land. As the rain fell, Elijah, overtaken by the power of the Lord, ran ahead of Ahab's chariot all the way to Jezreel.

You would think that with all these supernatural manifestations of God's Spirit at work, Elijah would get a little respect. But *nooo*, that evil queen Jezebel had the nerve instead to threaten his life! Her spirit of oppression spread throughout the land, gripping everyone with fear, including her husband, who yielded to whatever she wanted for fear of being confronted by her wrath. And now Jezebel was infuriated at the death of her lackeys, those false prophets of Baal she surrounded herself with. And her undesirable attention was now vindictively directed toward Elijah. Needless to say, this seriously dampened his exhilaration of calling down fire and rain from heaven. His victory felt short-lived as he ran for his life. He felt so isolated, so spent, so…depressed. How God could leave him at the mercy of this wicked woman was beyond him. Why hadn't God struck her down while He was on a roll? After all, Elijah had confronted God's enemies and wiped them out with a vengeance. Didn't one good favor deserve another?

And yet here Elijah was, fleeing for his life. Perhaps he was getting old. Maybe he couldn't take all this excitement anymore. With resignation closing in around him like heavy velvet curtains, he concluded he might as well die—he had definitely had enough. He was too tired to be startled by even the angel of the Lord who appeared to him, instructing him to eat. Almost in a dreamlike state, Elijah did as he was told, eating enough to strengthen himself to make the journey to Horeb, the mountain of God, driven by nothing more than the desire to get some sort of answer.

And then He was there…God, asking Elijah why *he* was there. How could God ask such a question? Didn't He know how hard Elijah had been working for Him? Didn't He know how badly the rest of the people were behaving? How they had persecuted and killed everyone who made a stand for God? Why, Elijah was the only one left. The only one who hadn't compromised his standards. The last one…and now they were trying to kill him!

He didn't know what to expect as the Lord invited him to stand in His presence on the mountain. At this point, facing the great and powerful wind that tore the mountain apart as well as the earthquake and fire that followed was better than facing Jezebel. But then came the gentle whisper of God, humbling him and asking once again, "What are you doing here, Elijah?" But Elijah missed the real question. "How could you ever feel alone after I've revealed My presence to you in such undeniable ways? Will you always need a major display to be convinced that you're not alone? Don't you know I'm bigger than the box you've put Me in? Don't you know that I am nearer to you in the stillness than I am in all outward manifestations? No, My son, you are not alone. You have reinforcement beyond what your eyes see and your senses conceive. You should have learned that lesson when you were waiting for Me to send the rain."

As Elijah descended from the mountain, reenergized, refocused, reassured, he felt renewed purpose. He had work to do. It was amazing the difference a conversation with God could make. How kind He was, always faithful to meet those who called out to Him at their point of need. Not only did He offer food for the body, He gave fortification to the soul.

How many times have you become weary of well doing when you see no immediate rewards in sight? We struggle even more when we suffer for righteousness' sake—especially when God doesn't seem to come against our enemies the way we feel He should. We can stand in bold, unwavering faith one moment and plummet to the depths of despair and doubt in a matter of seconds once the enemy of our souls rises up to retaliate against us. And we begin to take the spiritual warfare that ensues personally instead of remembering that we never stand alone. It is the One who is within us that the enemy hates. Therefore, an attack against us is an attack against God, and He takes it personally. For this reason we have

His promise that He is able to keep that which is committed to Him, for God defends His own. In that promise we can rest secure that no weapon the enemy fashions against us will ever prosper.

> *Dear Heavenly Father, in the middle of the fray it is easy to lose sight of Your arm defending me and Your hand sustaining me. When I hunger, feed me with Your Word. When I thirst, refresh me with Your Spirit. When I shiver in fear, warm me with Your consolation. Make Yourself more real to me than You've ever been when I wander alone in the wilderness. Remind me that when the arrows fly, my relationship with You will be my breastplate shielding me from Satan's attacks against my heart. Help me to constantly practice Your presence even when You are silent. Train me to hear Your whisper and walk in the unwavering confidence that You are with me always. In Jesus' name, amen.*

Journal about a time when you felt forsaken by the Lord. What was the range of emotions that you felt? When did He show up? What happened? What did you learn from the experience? What confession can you make about the faithfulness of God in light of your experience?

_____

_____

_____

_____

THE YIELDING TIMES

*The Lord provided a huge fish to swallow
Jonah, and Jonah was in the belly of the
fish three days and three nights.*

JONAH 1:17

Jonah had a sinking feeling that his stubbornness and rebellion had finally caught up with him. From the time God had told him to go to Ninevah, things had taken a turn for the worse. How could God ask him to go to Ninevah? *Ninevah*, of all places! Why should he even bother with those wicked people? Why give them a chance to repent? As far as he was concerned, they weren't even worthy of the chance to receive God's grace. They should be wiped out with one fatal swoop of God's arm. That would serve them right, and still be far too kind an act in Jonah's estimation. They were the most cruel, godless, horrific people on the face of the planet. And where they lived was a literal cesspool of filth and corruption. "Anything goes" was the mantra of Ninevah. Prostitution, witchcraft, murder in broad daylight. People just stepped over the dead bodies and kept on walking, unaffected by it all. These people were known for impaling on poles the heads of those they considered their enemies and parading them around for public sport.

And this is where God wanted him to go to call the land back to repentance? *Thanks a lot, God!* Jonah thought. He was literally being cast to the wolves. If that's as much as God thought about him, perhaps it was time Jonah took his life into his own hands. He was sorry, but no way was he going to risk his neck delivering a message to a scary bunch of people he didn't like anyway. With his luck, they would kill him and *then* repent. And God, being as softhearted toward the contrite as He was, would then turn and pardon them. Oooo, the very thought made Jonah grind his teeth. No way! Absolutely not! God had asked him to do some difficult things in his lifetime, but this was one time he just could not go along with the program.

Of course, who can run from the voice of the Lord and expect anything to go right? Yet Jonah was willing to test his tether. He thought perhaps God had let him off the hook because he was actually able to get on a boat headed to Tarshish. But it didn't take long to find out that God was quite serious about this Ninevah assignment. All of a sudden anxious hands roughly awakened him from a deep sleep. Awakened him to a real nightmare. "Wake up and call on your God. Perhaps He can save us!" someone cried out. The ship was being tossed to and fro on the sea like a balled-up piece of paper. Everyone was in a state of distress, babbling and calling out to whichever god they knew. At a time like this, who could be fussy? Whatever might work, they were willing to give it a try. They were throwing things overboard, and the entire place was up for grabs. In the midst of confusion, Jonah thought to himself, *All right, Lord.*

Jonah knew and the people on board knew that this whole mess was his fault. They had instinctively hesitated to allow him to sail with them when he had mentioned he was running from his God. After all, who had ever succeeded in such an undertaking? But Jonah had convinced them that his God only punished the guilty, and now here they were suffering on his account. But they would not jump to conclusions; they would instead cast lots and find out exactly who had brought all this trouble upon them. Upon Jonah's suggestion that he be thrown overboard, they did not want to appear too hasty. And so they resorted to their own human efforts to row the boat back to shore. Finally having to admit defeat, they reluctantly acquiesced to throwing Jonah overboard, and the sea resumed its calm.

Above on the ship, a fear of the Lord arose and the people blessed God and made a sacrifice to Him. Beneath the ship, sinking deeper into the sea, Jonah could do nothing but grudgingly admit to himself that this was another fine mess he had gotten himself into. Squirming in disgust as he was swallowed by a fish the Lord had prepared, he wondered if this wasn't some sort of cruel joke. Couldn't God just cut him a break? Why did He have to be so stubborn about this Ninevah thing? Well, two could play at this game. And so he sat in the dank belly of the fish and pouted…one, two, three days before beginning his dialogue with God. Knowing he was in no place to argue with God at this moment, Jonah finally conceded, "All right, who am I fooling? You and You alone are God. My fight with You is fruitless. My stubbornness has become an idol I've clung to, separating me from Your grace. You alone have the ability to save even me, O Lord. Here I sit with no power to redeem myself. Only You can do it. I was foolish to withhold my obedience from You; instead I should be offering You a song of thanksgiving for the privilege of being able to serve You." And once God saw that Jonah knew who was boss, He released him to carry out His initial order. He prophesied destruction to the city.

Much to the annoyance of Jonah, God did exactly what he thought He would do. The Ninevites panicked, proclaimed a fast, repented, and God forgave them! "Can you believe that?" Jonah mused. "He allows me to be thrown overboard and swallowed up in a fish for much less than the horrible things these people have done. And they simply cower once and He forgives them, just like that! How could God play me like that? Doesn't He know I could have been stoned for delivering a false prophecy to these people? I just don't get it. He doesn't let me get away with anything! And all around me everyone else gets away with murder. It's better for me to just die right now because this is a losing battle."

And so Jonah sat outside the city and waited…waited to see if God would do His own thing or go along with Jonah's program. After all, he did have a reputation to maintain here. But God had something greater in mind than Jonah's reputation that had nothing to do with his personal worth. This was not a contest between the righteousness of Jonah and the unrighteousness of the Ninevites, or between validating points of view, or even between rewarding the right and punishing the wrong. It was about addressing a need—a need for redemption. God was about the business of bringing thousands of people to the saving knowledge of what Jonah already knew. And like a wise father, He knew His child would understand later but for now He had to do what He had to do. And Jonah must learn obedience for obedience's sake.

I remember that when my brother Ian was an infant, every Sunday evening Ford Motor Company ran a television commercial announcing, "Ford has a better idea!" My little brother would get so excited. He would start jumping up and down rejoicing, "Mommy, mommy, Ford has a quacky idea!" No matter how much we tried to correct him, he insisted that Ford had a *quacky*, not a better, idea. Like Ian, sometimes we feel that our ideas are better than God's design, and well, that's just plain ol' quacky. We get indignant, outraged, even downright self-righteous when we don't see others getting the punishment we think they deserve. And then

God takes it one step further by suggesting that we *love* those who we don't approve of! Oh, the gall of it all! Doesn't He see what we see? We see so little of the big picture from our vantage point, and perhaps that's why we are limited to a "point of view."

But God has a better idea because He knows the end of the movie. As we make judgment calls based on what our flesh feels rather than what the Spirit of God sees, we struggle to change the storyline to accommodate our own happy ending. This is when the situations of life swallow us up and we hit bottom. We lie there writhing in our own refusal to cry "Uncle," hoping that God will give in. But He doesn't, and we feel forsaken. We mistake His lack of yielding to our program as a lack of love or understanding, and in His eyes one has nothing to do with the other. He simply knows what's best for all involved and refuses to limit the opportunity for all to partake of His grace.

Dear Heavenly Father, help me to remember that I am the child and You are the Father. Help me to yield to Your loving instruction, being obedient even when I don't fully understand Your heart. Help me to move in the quiet trust that You know what is best for all. In spite of my own preconceived ideas and prejudices, help me to always keep Your kingdom, versus my personal world, in view. Help me to remember that the same grace You now extend to others, You first extended to me, and it is only because of the blood of Your Son, Jesus, that I am counted worthy. There are no works of which I can boast that would suffice to pay for my redemption. Help me to rejoice in Your kindness toward others, understanding that Your love for them does not displace me, as Your love for me does not displace them but rather adds

*another thread to the tapestry of Your intricate, divine
design for Your kingdom. In Jesus' name, amen.*

What quacky idea of yours have you thought God should go
along with lately? What does His Word say about your attitude or
idea? What fears and disappointments does this situation uncover
for you personally? What steps do you need to take to reconcile
your heart to how God feels about the situation?

_____

_____

_____

_____

_____

Oh, Lord
Some things You speak
are too profound to share,
too sweet to repeat…
How I revel in our intimacy,
this our secret place
where You whisper things
for my spirit only to hear.
I find my delight
in the knowledge
that we are
co-spirators of Your plan.

IN THE MIDST
OF THE CROWD

THE DECISIVE TIMES

*Noah found favor in the eyes of the Lord...Noah
was a righteous man, blameless among the people
of his time, and he walked faithfully with God.*

GENESIS 6:8-9

Noah pounded the last peg into the hull of the ark, closed his
eyes, and thanked God. At last it was complete. It had taken
him one hundred and twenty years of steadfast obedience in the
face of ridicule, relentless questions, and taunts of disdain to complete this assignment. "Rain?" some had said, looking at him as
if he'd lost his mind. "What exactly is rain? How can water come
from the sky? It's never come from the sky before. Why should it
come now? And surely it would be impossible for so much water
to fall that it would warrant the building of this...monstrosity!"
They didn't know quite what to call this colossal ship. When he first
began building it, the onlookers took bets among themselves as to
how long it would take him to abandon this senseless project, but
year after year had gone by and Noah was still diligently working.
His obsession with impending doom had passed from ridiculous,
unwarranted fear to dementia as far as they were concerned. All
this talk of rain. What foolishness. Everyone knew that the earth
irrigated itself from the streams that flowed beneath it. That water
would actually fall in torrents from the sky in such massive doses
that all of mankind would be destroyed—what an absurd notion!

And on top of that, the nerve of Noah to think that he, along with
his family, were the only ones who would escape God's displeasure

if He did indeed choose to unleash His wrath upon society. Why couldn't he just live and let live like the rest of them did? All of this talk about God seemed to have a rather damaging effect on his psyche. If that was what walking with God was all about, they could do without this too-strict overseer. They had no time for Noah's doom and gloom. No time for being so prim and proper. Always crossing your spiritual t's and dotting your religious i's was far too laborious. It just required too much sacrifice and concentration to get this righteous thing down. Noah needed to relax, relate, release. Life was to be embraced fully, freely sampling every pleasure and becoming intoxicated with the fulfillment of your every lust and desire. Looking at Noah's life, they wondered where the reward or fun in righteousness was. If all you got out of pleasing God was getting stuck building a stupid ship for one hundred and twenty years and being the laughingstock of society, they wanted no part of it.

So they drank, made merry, and continued on with their lives, stopping by every now and again to see if Noah had tired of his building project yet. He was included in the sightseeing tour whenever relatives and friends came to visit. "Oh, yes, and you must see our local preacher. He's been building a ship forever! He claims that water is going to destroy us all. Isn't that a scream?" They could always count on Noah to provide a good laugh, at least when he wasn't making them uncomfortable with his convicting forecasts.

One day, Noah and his ark were once again the main topic of discussion at the wedding feast of his neighbor's daughter. Several guests commented on the uncommon darkness of the sky. Thick, dark clouds were rolling across the heavens, leaving angry marks upon the crisp, sparkling blue firmament that had previously promised to serve as the perfect canopy for this afternoon of celebration. It was almost as if God was frowning down upon them and every cloud was another wrinkle in His creased brow.

The animals were also behaving rather strangely, someone commented. They seemed…restless, nervous, as if alarmed by something their masters could not see. Flocks of birds soared frantically overhead, back and forth, as if trying to decide in which direction they could escape their invisible pursuer.

And then they felt it. At first it was as if someone had accidentally flicked a drop of water on them. But upon surveying those around them no guilty culprit was found. As a matter of fact, everyone was doing the same thing! They looked in dismay at their garments. One drop. Two drops. Three *large* drops…of water…but coming from where? Slowly their eyes turned upward as they realized indeed that water was falling from the sky. Before this phenomenon could sink in, the water began to descend in sheets, drenching them completely. At first they stood rooted to the spot, incredulous, looking from their cupped hands to the sky as if attempting to connect the water splashing upon them to its source. Finally the reality of the moment sank in. The mad scurrying that ensued as everyone ran for cover was lost on Noah, who was comfortably settled into his ark, closing the cage door on the last animal that had entered. He cast one last sad glance toward the outside world as the Lord shut the door.

"The old man was right!" they screamed, heading blindly in the direction of Noah's ark. "Perhaps he will allow us to come in," they said, ignoring the shame they should have felt for their past cruel comments. But upon reaching the ship, they found the entrance sealed. Their hearts sank with their shoes into the mud. "If this keeps up, we'll all die," they moaned as they leaned against the ship, trying to think of another alternative. And then, horror of horrors, the springs beneath the earth began to burst forth as well! With this the people beat a hasty retreat, deciding that their rooftops were their last resort. Why hadn't they listened to Noah? Who could have known that his ramblings would come to pass? Over the next forty days and nights, the water rose to claim its victims one by one until nothing was left except the ark floating on the face of the waters, carrying its precious cargo.

As the water subsided so did God's anger. Remembering Noah, who had found favor with Him because he never allowed his heart to stray in the direction of the masses, God let the heavens and the earth finally rest. Noah disembarked tentatively from his new home, not knowing what to expect beyond the world he had grown used to. It had been almost a year since he had set his feet upon solid ground. Stillness and serenity greeted him. As far as his eye could see, fresh vegetation was beginning to peek out from its hiding place. Was this what Adam had felt? Then again, Adam had no history to mar his enjoyment of all that God had created. Noah had memories of more grievous days, and he was looking forward to a new beginning. His first thought was to make a sacrifice unto the Lord. Everything else had been swept away, but there was still God. As the pungent aroma of an acceptable offering wafted toward the heavens, God wrote a new covenant promising faithfulness between Himself and all life on earth. Across the sky, His handwriting reflected the prisms of His majesty in the form of a brilliant rainbow. Never again, He promised, would He pour out His wrath in such a devastating fashion. Noah gratefully accepted this promise. And in his mind, the rain that others had looked upon as God's wrath, he actually saw as God's tears—tears shed weeping for a lost world. *Oh, that I might never cause You to weep again,* he thought. And before this inner cry was complete, God added yet another ring to His handiwork, as confirmation of His pledge.

"Eat, drink, and be merry today, for there's always tomorrow to get it right," seems to be the mantra of the day for most. Yet there are some of us who God has reserved unto Himself, struggling to maintain lives that will be pleasing to our Lord and King. As sin becomes more and more the norm and doing wrong becomes more of a casual pastime, it's easy to feel like the odd one out. But you're not out there alone. This is the place where God's favor and protection can be found. Like Mama always said, "Every dog has its day," and that is the truth. In God's economy, doing nothing for Him leaves you with nothing in the end. No guarantees of His faithfulness, provision, or protection when the hard times come. You're on your own. But for those of us who stand our ground when everyone else around us is slippin' and slidin', He shuts us in, shields us from the ravages of disobedience, and surrounds us with His peace.

Dear Heavenly Father, when it's hard for me to swim against the tide of popular reasoning, help me to stand fast in my obedience to You. Help me to constantly be transformed by the renewing of my mind. Feed me from Your Word with revelation and understanding, but most of all give me a heart that beats for You so that after all is said and done, I will walk in a way that pleases You. Not based on what I know, but Who I know. Not based on fear of the consequences, but based on my love for You. In Jesus' name I pray, amen.

When are you most tempted to go with the crowd, even when you know they are going in the opposite direction of God's plan for your life? What makes you stray from your God-given assignment? Make a list of your areas of struggle and present them to the Lord.

Ask Him to give you a promise of assurance that He will keep you. Record His answer to you from His Word.

_____

_____

_____

_____

_____

THE HATEFUL TIMES

*"Here comes that dreamer!" they said to each
other. "Come now, let's kill him and throw him into one
of these cisterns and say that a ferocious animal
devoured him. Then we'll see what comes of his
dreams." When Reuben heard this, he tried to rescue
him from their hands. "Let's not take his life," he said.*

GENESIS 37:19-21

Reuben was torn. On one hand he could relate to how his other brothers felt. Joseph *was* a spoiled brat, a little too cocky for his liking. If his little brother thought he would ever bow down to him, he had another thing coming! On the other hand, he thought that Simeon and the others were pushing the envelope a bit too far. How could they even speak of killing their own brother? Rough him up and teach him a lesson, maybe. But murder? That was over the top. He felt reluctant to say anything, knowing his brothers all too well. His objections would be met with accusations about Reuben's own questionable character. They would dredge up the whole incident about him sleeping with his father's concubine and end with a crescendo of condemnation, asking him who he was to try to make them feel guilty about anything.

This always made Reuben fold back inside himself, wondering if God would ever grant him an opportunity to redeem himself. He had sinned out of anger and pain. No one else seemed to notice the suffering he had witnessed in his mother's eyes every time his father, Jacob, had glanced lovingly in the direction of Rachel, his other wife. They hadn't watched their mother cry every time his father went into Rachel's tent to be with her for the night. Though his mother, Leah, and Rachel were sisters, all the children they produced were part of a contest, a desperate wager to gain Jacob's affections. As a boy, his mother had even sent him to gather mandrakes so that she might concoct a love potion, an aphrodisiac, to gain Jacob's amorous attention! It was an insult. An insult to his mother. He had seethed throughout his entire childhood.

His father had never felt the pain of being rejected, having something taken from him. He deserved to be hurt so that he could see how it felt. So what if it was a sin and a disgrace for Reuben to sleep with one of his father's women. It was a disgrace how Jacob treated Leah! So he flaunted his youth and virility in the face of Jacob's age. Yet his anger and pain had not subsided after lying in Bilhah's arms. No feeling of release came from the look of distress and hurt he saw in his father's eyes when Reuben's behavior was brought to his attention. As a matter of fact, he felt even deader dead than before. He concluded that he had imprisoned himself with his own lack of forgiveness, first for his father, and now for himself. He was not surprised that Joseph would be his favorite son. After all, he was born from Jacob's favorite woman. Reuben had taken the special treatment of his stepbrother in stride, though it often felt like sandpaper scraping across an old wound that was still festering.

As he hurried back to the cistern to retrieve Joseph and send him on his way, Reuben stopped with a start. Where was he? He could just see it now—here was something else he would be blamed for. And indeed he should be. He was the oldest. He should have pulled rank, taking a firmer stand against their abuse of Joseph. But now it was too late. He looked at his brothers with different eyes as they calmly wove their tale of deception about the death of

Joseph at the hand of wild animals. Who were these people? How could they sell their own brother into slavery? Was he the only one who had a conscience? They could degrade him, Reuben, as much as they pleased about what he had done in the past; he deserved it. But Joseph did not deserve this. And Jacob did not deserve this either, no matter what type of father or husband he had been. But Reuben went along with their plan, as he did with everything else they did, too weary to go against the flow any longer.

The news broke the old man when they returned home, and it broke something in Reuben that day too. All the anger he felt toward Jacob melted as his father's tears washed away all the residual bitterness that had built up over the years. But still fearing the repercussions, Reuben couldn't bring himself to tell Jacob the truth. Instead he worked out his guilt by extending himself as much as he could toward his father and Joseph's remaining younger brother, Benjamin. During the day he was the consummate caregiver to them. At night he fought his own demons as he experienced consuming nightmares of Joseph being tormented and calling to him. In the dreams he would try to rescue Joseph, but his brother was always out of reach. Time and time again he failed to be his salvation. And therefore he had none of his own.

Years passed and the famine came. They were struck hard, and Reuben felt he'd gotten his just desserts. But off to Egypt they went. He thought of how his brother had long ago gone down this same path as they journeyed past landmarks that reminded him all too well of that day. Upon reaching Egypt all the rest of the events became a swirling maze…snatches of reality breaking through…the tall stranger who seemed oddly familiar yet bore no resemblance to anyone he knew…the accusal of being spies…demanding Benjamin be presented as proof that they were not lying. This was where it had to stop; Reuben couldn't take any more. This time he didn't care what anybody had to say; he was going to take the bull by the horns and take responsibility. If need be, he would offer the lives of his own sons in exchange for Benjamin. This was his last chance to work out his own salvation, to try to silence his brother's blood from accusing him any further. So back to Egypt they went. Again the events blended together…being invited to this Egyptian's house for dinner…being seated in birth order…how did he know?…being accused of stealing!… Oh, would condemnation never feel its work was through? This was a worse nightmare than the one he had been having repetitively. And then the light broke…a moment of redemption more glorious than he ever had hoped for now arrived. Joseph was alive! Alive and well! Alive and well and a man of great influence in Egypt!

Now Reuben was relieved to bow at his brother's feet. Gone was the bile that had risen in his throat when Joseph predicted this moment so long ago. He was free. He felt as if he were being washed by rain as his own tears cleansed his soul and he begged for forgiveness. He would have given any amount of money, time and time again over the years, to be able to go back in time and report to Jacob that his favorite son was alive. To see the smile that came upon the old man's face at news more glorious than even the birth of his first son. The shackles that bound Reuben's soul fell off that day. God had not forsaken him; He had indeed been merciful to release him from his self-inflicted hell. Perhaps his past awful deeds and awful words could not be taken back, but God had extended His grace to him in the only way he could have ever regained his peace—by granting him one more opportunity to bring pleasure to his father's heart. Reuben knew there was only one way—through his son.

We've all met him and realized from experience that Condemnation is a brutal bully. He paralyzes us when we want to do right by reminding us of our past misdeeds: "Who do you think you are? How dare you get on your high horse after what you've done. Won't you look ridiculous trying to play the saint? *Everybody* knows what you're really made of!" That's usually enough to stop us dead in our tracks. Make us compromise standards we've thought better of. Discourage us from correcting someone else, lest our conscience remind us we're no better than they are. We're too busy stoning ourselves to stone the enemy. And yet God waits to exchange our sin and condemnation for the life of His Son. If He can make such a tremendous sacrifice, surely we can release a few bags we no longer need to carry.

> *Dear Heavenly Father, I've done some things in my life that I am so ashamed of. I feel that I might never break free of the accusing voices in my head. I wonder how You could love someone like me and if a second chance can ever be a reality. A clean, fresh start seems to be an elusive dream buried under the burden of my guilt. I struggle to release myself from my guilt, only to find myself sinking deeper into the quicksand of resignation that I will never be able to change. I find myself clinging to one solitary promise. He who the Son has set free is free indeed. Father, I reach out my hands to You; meet me in this place of failure. I call on You to free me from my sins. Even greater yet, free me from myself. Wash me, restore me, and help me to begin again. In Jesus' name I pray, amen.*

What things still burden you from your past? Which offenses do you repeatedly lay down only to pick back up again? What is the thought pattern that stands between you and God's forgiveness? Make a list of these things and offer them up to the Lord. Find a scripture verse to claim and meditate upon God's forgiveness toward you.

_____

_____

_____

_____

_____

THE IMPATIENT TIMES

When the people saw that Moses was so long in coming down from the mountain, they gathered around Aaron and said, "Come, make us gods who will go before us. As for this fellow Moses who brought us up out of Egypt, we don't know what has happened to him."

EXODUS 32:1

To be perfectly honest, Aaron had no explanation for the delayed return of his brother, Moses. He wished Moses had given him some idea of how long he was going to be gone. The masses were restless, and he was getting nervous. He was also growing weary of their constant complaining. They were never satisfied. Perhaps it was a habit they would never break. Aaron didn't know how the Lord felt about it, but he was sick of their attitude. You would think that by now they'd be convinced of the power of God. He had brought them out of Egypt, given them food, water, victory over Pharaoh's chariots...certainly that was enough! As far as he was concerned, God had proven Himself. But then again, the people were afraid of this God. Even Aaron had to admit He seemed a bit fearsome. When He descended to the foot of the mountain to speak with the people, they were afraid of His glory and fled. No longer willing to meet with God, they handed the task of message-bearer to Moses. They forfeited being in the presence of God and enjoying one-on-one communication with Him for secondhand "he said, God said" conversation. And now that Moses had gone to get the message they chose not to receive firsthand, they had the nerve to be upset because he was taking too long! Well, you just couldn't win for losing with these people.

Aaron was annoyed. Annoyed by a lot of things. On one hand, Moses expected him to be a leader on call. On the other hand, Moses was running everything: "Do this, do that." Aaron grumpily muttered under his breath as he reviewed his list of disappointments. By his estimation, his role was not clearly defined. Was he always to repeat whatever Moses told him God said he should say? He wanted to do some thinking for himself, not just carry out a bunch of orders. And that brought him back to his original quandary—Moses had left him "in charge" of these people who seemed to have no respect for anyone, including God. Now that they'd decided that Moses wasn't coming back, they thought they needed to create some other god to lead them. Well, wasn't that just too ironic? They didn't want to talk to the God they had; they merely wanted a more manageable model of Him. One that couldn't talk back. One that let them do as they pleased and blessed them anyway.

Who was he to argue with these people? Why should he put himself in personal danger, anyway? Moses was the one who was ultimately responsible for them all. Let him deal with them whenever—if ever—he returned. So Aaron ordered all of them to bring their gold earrings to him, and he gave them what they had been asking for, thinking that they would see the ridiculousness of it all once they compared an inanimate object with the glory of God's visitation at the mountain. But his plan backfired. The people actually got excited about this golden calf! Didn't they know it was just a collection of all their jewelry? They couldn't be serious! In a panic, Aaron tried to sway them back to the Lord by building an altar in front of the calf and decreeing a festival in honor of the Lord, but it was too late. The people were out of control. The golden calf was their cue to indulge themselves in pagan revelry.

They ate, they drank, they rose up to play and cast off their garments with wild abandon. Aaron watched and wondered how he would ever explain all of this to Moses.

He found out soon enough. Moses broke up the party with a bang. Casting down the tablets he had brought down the mountain with him, he headed straight for the golden calf with a rage in his eyes that surpassed any previous bursts of anger Aaron had witnessed in his headstrong brother. Aaron held his breath and waited for the explosion he knew would soon come his way after Moses dealt with the people. The people! It was their fault! Moses knew they were out of control when he left them in his brother's care. The spell over the entire camp broke as Moses melted down the golden calf, ground up the cooled gold, and forced the people to drink its shavings in water. Aaron, ashamed that he had allowed himself to be intimidated by the unbelieving masses, found it difficult to even confess that he had made the golden calf. So he lied, "All I did was throw the jewelry into the fire, and this calf came out. Come on, Moses. Cut me a break. Even you have trouble with these people!" But Moses only looked at him and sadly shook his head, as if confronting an incorrigible child, before turning back to the scrambling Israelites who were now being put to death in the camp.

When the furor at last subsided in the camp, Moses related to his brother what had happened on the mountain. All of Aaron's rationale and self-justification went out the window, leaving room for true contrition in his heart. While Aaron was down below feeling alone, cut out of the picture, he had been very much on God's mind. While he was feeling ignored and underrated, God was securing his position down to the details of how he would be dressed and exactly what his job description would be. While he was feeling completely insignificant in the scheme of things, God was stressing how important Aaron would be in the order of conducting the affairs of the priesthood. Tears of repentance flowed as he realized he had been just like the people he judged. Unbelieving. Foolish and self-consumed. Aaron finally realized what Moses already knew—that the only way he could find his own worth and overcome all he had been feeling was to find himself in the presence of God.

Sad to say, many of us are guilty of feeling forgotten by God at the exact same time He sits in heaven rubbing His hands in glee over a blessing that He's busy preparing for us. When we have no visible proof of God at work in our lives, it is difficult to remember that we are very much on His mind, still very much a part of His active agenda. We forget that we are called to walk by faith and not by sight. We begin to yield to the arm of flesh. We become irritable and defensive when questioned about our actions. "Well, God didn't say anything, and I had a peace about it," we retort shortly. But where is that peace now? When we're caught in the throes of impatience, anything that drowns out the immediate longing of the flesh will give us momentary peace. Satan is always happy to hand us grease to put on the burn, knowing it will bring brief comfort before causing further damage and pain. But the peace that passes all understanding is found in keeping your mind on the One who is always thinking of you—Jesus.

Dear Heavenly Father, far too many times I have been tempted to take matters into my own hands when I don't see You coming through according to my schedule.

I succumb to pressure from the expectations of those around me and resort to trying to make things happen myself. Please forgive me for the moments of murmuring and doubt that I entertain when things aren't going the way I would like them to go. Silence my fears and my doubts with Your Word. Let the Holy Spirit bring Your promises back to my remembrance and speak peace to my soul. Increase my trust in You and help me to stand fast knowing that though I cannot see physical evidence in the times I feel forsaken, You are very much present and active in my life. In Jesus' name I pray, amen.

What areas do you feel God has forsaken you in? What areas do you think God is moving too slowly in? What do you think contributes to your lack of trust in God? What can you do to reestablish faith in the areas where you question God's interests? Write a confession you can stand on from God's Word to refresh your hope.

THE RISKY TIMES

*Joshua spared Rahab the prostitute, with her
family and all who belonged to her, because she
hid the men Joshua had sent as spies to Jericho—
and she lives among the Israelites to this day.*

JOSHUA 6:25

Rahab closed the door behind the last customer and leaned against it in utter fatigue. Her spirit was tired. Her soul ached more than her body as she blinked back tears of frustration. Though her home was a place of "solace" for many a stranger and traveler, she felt isolated and lonely. She had made a profession out of relieving others' "needs," and yet she felt so empty. Who was there to relieve her? She tipped up her chin as if to reinforce her resolve that a woman's got to do what a woman's got to do in hard times. There was no one to take care of her. It was up to her to survive as best she could, much to the chagrin of her family. Their disappointment in her was apparent, and it seemed as if she had no way to redeem herself in their eyes—or in her own, for that matter. But she refused to be the victim. At least she wasn't out there begging. She worked for what she had, whether or not it was considered a legitimate profession. But in moments when she let down her guard, like tonight as she leaned out her window gazing long into the night and observed the serenity of the moon and the stars, she wondered if there was really a God. And if there was, would He ever take pity on someone like her? Was it possible for Him to deliver her from her circumstances?

Her gaze shifted downward, from the perfect black canopy that seemed to be adorned with diamonds suspended and shimmering as far as she could see, to the plains where it was rumored that the Israelites lay in wait, considering when best to seize Jericho. She had heard of their God and how He fiercely fought battles on their behalf. The entire city was in a state of alarm awaiting what they speculated would be certain destruction. What did you have to do to get a God like that on your side? Rahab didn't know how long she stood there pondering her fate, daring to dream of better days, before she finally closed the shutters. Whispering a prayer to whoever cared to hear, she descended into an unusually peaceful sleep.

Upon waking Rahab thought for a fleeting moment about how well she had slept—the best sleep in as long as she could remember, in fact. Usually the night was filled with troubling dreams of someone chasing her, dragging her somewhere she didn't want to go. Often she would awake drenched in sweat, trembling like a leaf. But this morning was different; she was actually refreshed. The people in the market eyed her strangely as she hummed to herself while making her rounds, gathering provisions for the day. *What is with Rahab?* she imagined them wondering. She usually sauntered through with her head held high, her face set in an emotionless mask that seemed to dare anyone to look at her in a judgmental fashion. But today, well, Rahab actually smiled!

The rest of the day passed no differently than any other, and eventually gave way to dusk. The same familiar knock came at the door, but totally unfamiliar faces stood before her when Rahab opened it. She could tell from their countenances that they were foreign; she knew by instinct that they were Israelites. Closing the door quickly behind her, she asked them to state their business, noting that they did not look like the type who were in search of her services. As they explained themselves, she knew intuitively that she must help them. Perhaps this was her last chance to escape this life if truly the city was doomed. Maybe their God would give her a chance. It was worth the risk. She could become no more an outcast than she was already. Before Rahab had finished securing their hiding place on the roof, another knock, even more urgent than the first, came. This time the king's messengers stood before her with shifty eyes, signaling for her to behave as if she didn't recognize them. They demanded that she hand over her visitors, for they were spies who would put them all in danger. Though her heart was beating wildly, she maintained her practiced blank face that was completely unreadable, informing them that the spies had left long before the closing of the city gate. Studying her face for any hint of a lie for a suspended instant in the light of the torch they carried, they concluded she would be of no further help, and they departed.

After letting the spies down through her window, Rahab secured the scarlet cord that would be her salvation in the window as she had been instructed. Again she looked heavenward. Was He really up there? "If You are, please deliver me from this nightmare," she breathed.

Over the next several days Rahab tried to pass the time as usual, but everything had changed. She now had hope. She waited until the Israelites arrived. Somberly they came, marching soundlessly around the city gates. One day, two days, three days…the silence was deafening, the tension unbearable. The entire city waited with its breath held as day after day they marched, waiting for what, no one knew. Rahab timed her visit to her family's house at a time when she knew their nerves would be too raw from fear to waste their energy on disapproving of or resisting her invitation. She knew they would be ready to embrace any solution she offered, and she was right. Willingly they sought the refuge of her home, though most people had abandoned the houses on the wall, fearing they would be attacked first. Huddled together waiting, they drew measured breaths and strained to hear into the silence as the Israelites continued their interminable march, the trudging sound they made becoming more ominous with each step. Suddenly trumpets sounded and battle cries filled the air! Rahab could feel the walls collapsing and with them her consciousness also collapsed. Strong arms lifted her, carrying her through the rubble along with the rest of her family and setting her feet on a solid rock some distance away from the chaos. She sank to the ground, weeping, thanking a God who was more merciful than she had hoped. He had saved her and her household. She had also been redeemed in the eyes of her family. And because God blessed her while she was yet unpleasing, she, in turn, would seek to please Him all her days.

There are times in our lives when, so deep is our sin in our own eyes, we are sure that God stands far off along with the rest of those who disapprove of the things that we've done. Rejection, shame, and condemnation choke out any hope we have of forgiveness, redemption, or blessing. We are almost afraid to utter a plea for help, fearing God's certain rebuttal. Yet even the most timid voice, trembling with hope the size of a mustard seed, reaches His ears, and His response is immediate—not with wasted words but with life-saving action, so happy is He that you called. For those of us humbled by our own state of unworthiness, He supplies abundant grace.

Dear Heavenly Father, my sin is too much for me
to bear. I have no one to turn to but You. All others

*have forsaken me, and though I feel as if I am
drowning in unworthiness, I pray You will hear my
cry. Only You can restore me and mend my heart. I
ask that You would forgive me and grant me a new
beginning as I choose to follow You. Grant me Your
Holy Spirit to be my guide and help me to remain
steadfast. Cleanse me, fill me, teach me, and lead me
in the way of life everlasting. In Jesus' name, amen.*

What sins do you struggle with that make you feel unworthy
of God's assistance? Confess those things to Him. Find scriptures
on forgiveness to meditate on. Write a confession of God's forgiveness for you to establish in your heart.

_____

_____

_____

_____

_____

THE DECIDING TIMES

*Because my servant Caleb has a different
spirit and follows me wholeheartedly, I will
bring him into the land he went to.*

NUMBERS 14:24

Caleb couldn't believe his ears. When would these people ever learn? He felt the desire to shout at the top of his lungs, "You idiots! How long will you maintain this pathetic slave mentality that you can't have more than what you already possess, for heaven's sake?" All the way back from the land they'd gone to check out, Caleb was tingling. It was hard for him to walk normally. He was literally vibrating with the desire to leap and somersault all the way home. After all they had been through, this was truly worth it. God was so awesome! What a land—it literally flowed with milk and honey! The fruit was so lush that it took two men to carry a branch of grapes! It was as if God had multiplied everything in the land to make up for their time of lack and suffering. He couldn't wait to move in. And now here were these men causing needless alarm with their negative report. So what if they'd seen giants! Hadn't God delivered them from their enemies before? What was so new about this exercise? Caleb's heart sank as the moans from the crowd grew louder. He cast a glance toward Joshua, who looked as perturbed as Caleb felt. Were they the only two who believed?

Caleb pressed forward. He didn't care what they thought; he would speak his mind. "I believe we should go up and take the land. We can do it," he stated. The others bristled at his confident words, but he would not be dissuaded. He was sick of their limited mentality. Sick of their incapability to give God the honor He was due. It was downright offensive…insulting…disrespectful how they carried on every time God instructed them to do something. Caleb had a mind to leave them right there and go into the new land without them. As far as he was concerned, they didn't deserve to go if their faith in God was so miniscule. Who needed them? He didn't want to be associated with their mindset. If he was the odd man out, that was fine with him. It was hard to believe he and these people came from the same place. They saw things so differently! At first Caleb thought something was wrong with him, but when he meditated on the goodness of God, rehearsing all he had seen Him do, everything made sense. Joshua, who had spent time with the Lord in the tabernacle, had discussed this with Caleb while they were away. It seemed a repeat of when the people drew back from having individual contact with God and instead assigned Moses to bring them messages. They missed out on understanding the fullness of who He was. And therefore they struggled to trust Him constantly.

Caleb was snatched back from this train of thought by frantic voices surrounding him. The more the people mumbled, the more grieved he became. Stoning? How could they speak of stoning them? He didn't know if it was grief or madness that caused Joshua and him to begin rending their garments. The insolence of the people in the face of what God desired to do for them was heartbreaking. He could only hope that God would accept his personal apology for their disgraceful behavior. Caleb, who had followed God wholeheartedly from the time he was a child, could not relate to this blatant lack of faith. He delighted in worshiping the Lord and beholding His glory as He led the people toward the Promised Land. He believed that nothing was impossible with God. After all, he had seen Him at work. Taking possession of what already belonged to them according to the Word of God, who could not lie, was nothing compared to what they had been through already.

As he waited for Moses to return from consulting with God, his mind raced to try to anticipate God's reaction to this episode of chaos in the camp. He found out soon enough. And what happened was more horrifying than he imagined, but nothing within him could find a reason to argue with God's verdict. The other men who had gone to spy out the land, with the exception of Joshua and himself, were killed in a plague that silenced their bad report. But the worst part of all, the part Caleb and Joshua couldn't escape, was the punishment handed down to the rest of the people. They would not enter the land of promise at all. They had chosen the fate of wandering in the desert for another forty years until all of them died with their foolish words. Their children would enter Canaan, but every man and woman who had been filled with unbelief could go no further than what he or she believed. Caleb and Joshua would be allowed to go in, but they would have to wait until the new generation—the children of this generation—went in. It was excruciating to bear the weight of the others' disobedience, but Caleb comforted himself with the knowledge that God would reward his faithfulness by keeping him so that he and his descendants could claim their inheritance.

Now, forty-five years later, much had come to pass. Moses had died, Joshua now led the people, and the campaign to claim what was theirs was well underway. Caleb was now eighty-five, yet just as strong as he was on the first day that God had spoken of giving them this territory. Caleb stood before his friend and leader, Joshua, and said with the kind of boldness that comes only when you know you're backed by God, "Give me this mountain." He had never been one to run from a battle, and was ready to claim what belonged to him. The thought of a good fight right about now was rather stimulating to him. He relished the opportunity to vanquish the Lord's enemies. With Joshua's permission, Caleb set off, a purpose in his step, feeling the exhilaration of at last being in the center of God's divine will.

Isn't it a relief to know that no matter what, God's plan for your life will be intact? As long as you're willing to follow Him wholeheartedly, He remains a faithful partner even when all others bail out. Though the unbelief and negativity of those around us can cause delays in what we're ready to embrace immediately, fortunately God remains true to His Word. He marks the spot with your name and preserves what is yours to claim until the day of fulfillment. We can find peace in what seems to be a delay by remembering that as children of God we are never victims of circumstance—only participants in a plan much greater than our finite understanding, a plan in which every detail has been painstakingly worked out in God's omniscient way that culminates in His perfect timing.

Dear Heavenly Father, so many times I feel that my life or my circumstances have been put on hold because of things beyond my control. Please forgive me for forgetting that You still reign. Help me to keep my eyes on You, following You with all my heart, mind, and soul, even when the masses are going in another direction. As I meditate on Your promises, make them come alive inside of me, that I might not be swayed by doubt, delay, or

*what my eyes see, but only by what Your voice speaks. I
pray that I never treat Your promises with contempt
but rejoice in all You say and do on my behalf. Keep
me sensitive to Your voice that I might move quickly
and obediently at Your command. I claim my blessings
now according to Your promise. In Jesus' name, amen.*

Make a list of blessings that you feel have slipped through your
fingers because of the intervention or lack of participation by others.
Which ones did God promise you? Write a promise from His Word
next to the item on your list that it matches. Surrender your timing issues and ask God to grant you the gift of faith to believe again.

_____

_____

_____

_____

_____

It is in the valley,
in the alone
that we find ourselves
in the best of company…
this is the place where
God fills all the empty spaces
for He has finally been
given the room to do
what He does best…

THE TRANSITIONAL TIMES

*Ruth the Moabite said to Naomi, "Let me go
to the fields and pick up the leftover grain
behind anyone in whose eyes I find favor."*

RUTH 2:2

Ruth arched her back, stretching out the kinks, bringing some relief to her aching muscles. As she turned slightly from side to side to ease the tension in her waist, she saw a small cluster of male workers looking in her direction. In the center of the cluster was a distinguished older man who was studying her with great interest. She hoped she wasn't trespassing on the wrong field. Her understanding was that she was free to glean behind the workers in the field. This was the law of their God—widows and others less fortunate were free to take whatever was left behind in the harvest.

How kind this God is to be so compassionate in His provision for all people, Ruth thought to herself. This was one of the reasons why she chose to follow Naomi, her mother-in-law, back to Bethlehem from Moab. After her husband, Naomi's son, had died, there was no reason to remain in Moab. Nothing tugged at her heart strongly enough to keep her there. She had grown to love not only her husband but his entire family. She loved their quiet faith and their considerate ways. She was intrigued by their God, this God who had delivered their people from slavery and brought them to a land of promise. As they rehearsed their story over the Passover meal year after year, her mind was filled with images of the death angel passing over their ancestors' houses in Egypt. Of Pharaoh and his army being drowned in the Red Sea. Of a God who led them by fire at night and by a cloud during the day. Who rained down food for them to eat and fiercely fought their enemies. Their God was nothing like the silent idols the people worshiped in Moab. Ruth had long wondered if they really heard her petitions and if the events of her life came about more by happenstance than by design, yet they were all she'd had until she met her husband and learned differently. And then he died. His brother died. His father died. She ached for Naomi as she watched her mother-in-law's faith die with the birth of such hard circumstances. Though Ruth wasn't sure that their God, this Yahweh, would have her, she vowed to have enough faith for both of them and that she would be God's arms to Naomi until she was ready to embrace Him again.

It was hard for Ruth to believe that this God she had heard so much about would abandon His people just like that. Surely He would find a way to redeem their tragedy. She would not give up on Him, even if Naomi had. So on she went with Naomi to Jerusalem, leaving all she knew behind, ready to embrace this God if He would embrace her. She felt as free as the wind that coursed through her hair as she collected the stray barley. The sun…the fresh air…she couldn't explain it, but she had such a peace, such a sense of well-being. She enjoyed her time in the fields as much as she enjoyed her evenings spent talking with Naomi, chuckling at memories of pleasant yesterdays or learning new tidbits of information from Naomi's old friends who dropped by to catch her up on all she had missed in her absence. But now Ruth felt a strange stirring in her soul. She could still feel the eyes of that man on her as she turned back to her work. She knew that her people were enemies of Israel, which made her a woman who was vulnerable to attack. So she prayed silently to this God she had come to admire for favor and protection.

A shadow fell across Ruth's path causing her to look up. *What kind eyes he has*, she thought. Not quite knowing what to say, she waited for him to speak. Truly God had taken pity on her, for here this man was extending himself in a most generous manner, offering her water, lunch, the refuge of his fields to glean in under his care. Wait until she told Naomi! Surely this would lift her faith. That it did, and more. Naomi was quick to see this as an opportunity to replace all that Ruth had lost. Ruth wasn't sure she had that much faith, but she chose to yield in respectful obedience to Naomi. It was worth doing as she said just to see the gleam in Naomi's eyes. It had been a long time since her mother-in-law had looked forward to anything; who was Ruth to disappoint her? So off to the threshing floor she went with her heart in her hands, praying to Yahweh that this kind gentleman, Boaz, would not find her proposal presumptuous.

Ruth didn't know if it was the chill of the night air or her nervousness that made her shiver so as she lay down at his feet and waited for him to discover her. Would he be willing to be her redeemer? Or would he find her—a foreigner, an outsider, an insignificant victim of circumstance—unworthy of redeeming? And then came the surprise in the middle of the night. Yes, yes, he counted it a privilege to be her redeemer, and he was willing to do whatever he had to do in order to secure this covenant!

As she returned home bearing six measures of barley in her arms and praises to this wonderful God in her spirit, she pondered this sudden turn in her fate. And she found nothing to attribute it to but Yahweh. Naomi's faith resurfaced in leaps and bounds as Ruth related the story of how Boaz had agreed to make sure the matter would be settled. The wait was not a long one, and redeem her he did. Ruth's heart felt as if it would burst with the news. She had been bought with a price, redeemed, betrothed, made worthy, restored! She was no longer a foreigner; she had been grafted into a divine family tree. This God who had once been far away had drawn nigh and poured out His mercy on her in bountiful measure, giving credence to her faith and a home to her wandering soul. As she looked from the face of her loving husband to their newborn child in her arms, this child who would be the grandfather of King David and part of the lineage of Jesus Christ, she thought of Orpah, her sister-in-law who had turned back to Moab, and wept. She wept as she pondered the emptiness of a life lived without redemption and the gratitude she felt for how God had redeemed her own life.

Sometimes we are tempted to think we are further away from God than we really are. Faith feels like a foreign country. And hope is but a vague memory of a better frame of mind. We feel that the circumstances of life and its inevitable hardships are proof of His distance. Perhaps we are not so important in the scheme of things. Perhaps His time would be better spent on those more worthy of His notice, those who have an "in" with Him, those who have done exploits for His name's sake. Yet our hearts cry out for a redeemer to relieve us of our questions and our aloneness. To make us feel wanted, cherished, like we belong. And God comes bearing much more than we ever asked or hoped for. He comes bearing gifts of restoration that affirm who we are as well as where we're going. He wraps His arms around us and weaves our days into the tapestry of His divine design, making us into something beautiful, something good, something better than before.

Dear Heavenly Father, the transitions of life sometimes take their toll on my faith, causing me to question

*where I really stand with You. In those times I pray
that You draw near and reassure me of Your presence
and Your favor. As I try to find my way through the
foreign nuances of where change takes me, please be the
one familiar thing that I can cling to. Grant me Your
promise that You will meet me in this strange place
where I don't know what to do and point the way to
solid ground. Order my steps and establish me in the
midst of Your divine purposes. Fulfill Your plans for
me according to Your promise. In Jesus' name, amen.*

Do you struggle with feelings of unworthiness and feeling forsaken? Where do you feel that God has dealt harshly or unfairly with you? List the items in your life that cause you to struggle with your faith. Can you offer these things back to the Lord? Write a faith confession, not of the circumstance you were believing for, but based on who God is and what He's done for you in previous situations that tested your faith in order to build it back up stronger than ever.

THE TIMID TIMES

*And Kish said to Saul his son, Take now one of the
servants with thee, and arise, go seek the asses.*

1 SAMUEL 9:3 KJV

Saul stood surveying the land with furrowed brow, annoyed at this task and also at his failure to accomplish so trivial a mission. Chasing donkeys! This was not what he had been created to do. Why his father insisted that this was all that Saul was up to doing was beyond him. He heaved a heavy sigh; it was downright frustrating. From the time he was born, his father treated him as if he were too delicate for real man's work. He heard constant comments about how fair of face he was. He was taller than everyone else and therefore had been the source of ridicule among the other children—out of envy, his father said. But in his heart Saul knew that one day they would all see him in a different light. He didn't quite know how, but time would tell. Just because he was handsome did not mean he couldn't be as fierce a warrior as any other man. His father was known as a valiant man. This was his heritage. One day Saul would show them all a side of himself they hadn't anticipated.

Up one hill and down the next, with no donkey in sight. After three days, Saul grew weary of this fruitless chase and decided to turn back lest his father became concerned for his welfare. But his servant suggested that they visit Samuel the seer and enlist his help, so Saul decided to go a little further. Perhaps this seer could tell them something that would redeem this boring escapade in some way before they headed back. And if he could help them locate the wandering animals, all the better.

But who can ever anticipate a day like this day, when everything in your life is set on a track you never anticipated, and your world is never the same again? Though Saul had longed to be taken seriously, the words that Samuel said to him were astonishing. King over Israel! How could that be? He was torn between elation and fear. Amazement and understanding. Samuel had said that the power of the Lord would come upon him and he would become a different person. For this he was grateful. He would need all the help he could get. Even though he had always longed for recognition as a man of true stature, now that the moment was upon him, he couldn't really say that he felt ready for it. He had been pampered; he had led an easy life. He was spoiled. And though everyone said he was the most handsome man they had ever seen, he was still just a Benjamite. And not just a Benjamite—he was from the smallest clan of the smallest tribe in Israel. Who was going to take him seriously as king? But Samuel assured him that in seven days, all he said would be fulfilled.

Saul had to admit that he did feel different as he went on his way. As the company of prophets surrounded him, the Spirit of the Lord came upon him and he began to prophesy. The word spread quickly. No one could believe it—Saul was prophesying! What had come over him? This was a side of him they had never seen. He was always so low-key—shy, as a matter of fact. He did his best to avoid the stares of those who did a double take when they saw him. Many were moved to comment on how incredibly handsome he was, and they marveled at his height—a whole head taller than everyone else in the land! While all of this would have caused some to become haughty and self-absorbed, Saul became more introverted, more self-conscious. But here he was prophesying with abandon. *Since when did he get religion?* they wondered. They had never heard him say much of anything, period. And now here he stood delivering the Word of God. Well! Would wonders never cease?

And now here came Samuel, declaring that the Lord was ready to select the king that they had requested. And who did He select but this same Saul! Now the fear of failure rose up to engulf Saul. Perhaps he had been a bit hasty in his own self-assessment. So, while everyone was looking for him, he hid himself among the baggage. Some king! Yet he was the one that was crowned. The people just didn't understand God's reasoning in this matter at all. Why would He select Saul, of all people? Yes, he looked the part outwordly, but as far as they could see he was a pretty house with no one home. While some wandered away, murmuring that they were more doomed than ever before, Saul kept silent. He would show them. He would show them all.

The new king had to admit that, though Samuel had crowned him, he felt no different. So back to tending the fields he went, until the day the Ammonites besieged Jabesh Gilead. As the people wept and mourned their fate, Saul was filled with righteous indignation. Before he gave any thought to cautioning himself, the heart of a king rose up within him like the ire of a lioness protecting her cubs. So fierce was he in his call to arms that no one doubted that the Spirit of God was indeed upon him to lead the people. In the midst of routing the enemy, it finally hit Saul—this was what he had waited for all his life! A moment like this. God had heard the silent cry of his heart that he had found so difficult to express. He felt as if his desire had been buried beneath the weight of other people's doubts and his own insecurities, and it seemed as if some divine hand had cleared away all of the garbage to give him this one shot to demonstrate what he truly held within himself.

Charging across the field after the enemy, Saul felt liberated. Liberated to understand that in and of himself, he would never be anything more than a prisoner of his own fears, but with God as his source, he could accomplish anything. God had given him the victory when no one else saw his potential. This humbled him. Saul felt no need to hold a grudge against his naysayers, for the truth he now clung to with both hands was too precious to let go of. God would always be his defense. This was more than enough reason to forgive and forget. It was time to celebrate.

Though most people have heard the old adage that you can't judge a book by its cover, many people still do. They draw assumptions based on our appearance, and voice their conclusions without stopping to consider the damage their words may cause. And then God shows up and validates our existence by setting us apart for a purpose that no one expected us to fulfill. And though respect doesn't come immediately, it does come as God's favor goes before us to set the stage for our entrance. We find ourselves as surprised as those around us once we see all that we can accomplish through His strength and wisdom flowing through us. And the rejections of the past prepare us to be gracious hosts of the blessings now at hand.

Dear Heavenly Father, though I struggle with many insecurities and self-inflicted limitations, I long to be all that You created me to be. Help my faith to press past the doubtful opinions of others until I reach the place of Your endless possibilities. As I remember that it is Christ in me who accomplishes all things, help me to resist the

*urge to draw back in fear when You are beckoning me
onward. Grant me courage. Give me strength to run
the race as I choose to press toward the mark for the
prize of Your high call in Christ Jesus. Enable me to
apprehend that for which You have apprehended me.
And may all the praise I receive be as incense before Your
throne as I give it back to You. In Jesus' name, amen.*

What have been the secret aspirations of your heart? Why have you buried them? What stops you from grasping your dreams? How does your opinion of yourself differ from God's opinion of you? What promises can you find in His Word concerning your purpose? Make note of these and meditate on them.

_____

_____

_____

_____

_____

THE ACCOUNTING TIMES

Nathan said to David, "You are the man!
This is what the LORD, the God of Israel, says."

2 SAMUEL 12:7

Nathan paced back and forth in his room, as if the brisk walking would somehow erase the word of the Lord that was like a fire in the midst of his chest. How could he deliver such a harsh word to the king? He was just a prophet. It was one thing to be sent to deliver comforting words, or words of instruction on how to proceed in warfare against their enemies. But this message was a whole universe away from the usual message he was asked to carry to King David. This was personal. This was embarrassing and shameful. Adultery! He couldn't believe it, but then again he had to, because God never lied. Yet how could he handle this delicate matter without incurring the wrath of David and those around him? The people liked David, and with good reason. The land was at peace. The economy was good. He was a fair king. He was handsome and down-to-earth. Why, he had danced out of his clothes before the Lord while celebrating a hard-won victory! He was every man's king. Full of compassion and love for God and country.

Why David had been so foolish as to take another man's wife and then have the man killed was perplexing to Nathan. Ah, but there was the child she bore! David's child. Nathan surmised the king had to cover his tracks. But did he forget that God was watching? Did he really think that this holy God would entertain, then cover, his sin? What was David thinking? This was exactly why he should have gone to war with his people, but no, David had to stay at home. What a mess! And now he, Nathan, had been instructed to go and call him on the carpet. How would he even begin to broach the subject?

Nathan took his time, putting off his task as long as he could just in case God changed His mind and decided to deal with David privately. But now the burden had grown increasingly unbearable. Indeed, he must go. As Nathan walked toward the palace, his heart was heavy. Barely acknowledging the respectful nods he received along the way, he stayed focused on his present dilemma. His pain increased as he gazed upon David, who was always so happy to see him. "What shall I say, Lord?" he breathed the question as a silent prayer while continuing to search David's face for some sort of sign… something that reassured him that he wouldn't have to go any further, but all he saw was David's face filled with anticipation, waiting to hear what Nathan had to say. And so he began by weaving an intriguing tale about the victimization of a poor man by a man of privilege. He decided he would let David judge himself in the light of this allegory, for he was merely a messenger and not the magistrate.

David pronounced his judgment on the man in Nathan's story: repayment of property and death.

Then Nathan spoke: "The man is you."

David's heart dropped as he heard Nathan's words. The judgment he pronounced would also be his own. He too would pay fourfold for his sin. Calamity would not depart from his house. His own wives would be taken in broad daylight by someone close to him. The child would die in order to preserve the name of the Lord in the sight of His enemies and waylay their contempt. As David threw himself on the mercy of God, Nathan could only encourage him to ask for God's forgiveness; the consequences would remain.

This was the part that was hard for Nathan. He loved David. He knew that the king's heart was tender toward God. He hated to see him suffer this way. Hated the disappointment and pain it inflicted on his family and household. Hated that the country had to live under the shame of its leader's mistake. But sin is sin, no matter who commits it. The silence in the halls was deafening as Nathan made his way back down the corridor and out into the open air. He felt as if his lungs would burst. Had he been holding his breath the entire time? He went home, and he waited. He prayed for David. Prayed that God's mercy would be sufficient cause for him to endure this harsh punishment like an obedient son. Prayed that God would comfort him in a special way. "Restore what he has lost, O God. Let him know that You reward a heart that is tender toward You," Nathan prayed. He dared to hope that God would show David some tenderness in the midst of this terrible experience.

And then Nathan thanked God. Thanked God that he knew Him. Thanked God that He trusted him to bear His Word, no matter how harsh it may be at times, and never sent him alone. The Lord accompanied him with the spirit of conviction. The reward for Nathan was seeing those who chose to hear restored to wholeness. Only obedience and the tender mercies of a loving God could put the pieces back together of a life shattered by sin.

And then the news came that Bathsheba would bear another son. One whom God would love. Nathan chuckled to himself. Yes, it was just like God to graciously send him back to the palace—this time bearing good news.

Being the bearer of truth when others are running for cover is not the most desirable position to have, even when we're dealing with church folks. Saved or not, the truth hurts and can bring unpredictable reactions when the bearer of the message touches on a sensitive subject. Sometimes we watch as friends and family members make terrible decisions that we know will long affect their lives, and we wrestle to decide whether we should blow the whistle or keep the peace. But God urges us to speak the truth in love and allow His spirit of conviction to do the rest. It is not our job to render judgment on the offender. We are just to deliver the message, knowing that in the face of truth God always has our backs.

> *Heavenly Father, thank You for the gift of truth, for Your truth sets us free. Help me to remember this when I need to make a stand for Your Word instead of allowing those around me to continue going astray in their sin. Keep me mindful that true love is tough love, which is willing to sacrifice in order to save. Help me not to fear their reactions more than the judgment that will fall on their lives. Let the desire for righteousness always prevail over all else in my heart. Grant me the sensitivity to know when to speak and when to remain silent. I want to be ever sensitive to Your Spirit, and obedient to Your leading. In Jesus' name, amen.*

What incidences have you let slide in the past that you regret never speaking up about? Did you learn from those experiences? What are some steps you can take in order to present correction or concerns to others in godly fashion?

THE PROVING TIMES

Elisha...took the cloak that had fallen from
Elijah and struck the water with it. "Where now
is the LORD, the God of Elijah?" he asked.

2 KINGS 2:13-14

From the moment Elijah approached him in the fields, Elisha knew his life would never be the same, and he was ready. Ready to bid his family farewell. Ready to follow after God. His was a restless spirit that could not be contained in the mundane affairs of everyday life; his spirit thirsted for more. More of what God had. More power to experience the supernatural. More than what others sought. So willingly he followed Elijah, but not in pursuit of just an ordinary call. Zealously he served, gleaning all he could from Elijah's words as well as his example. Elisha stored up all that he saw and heard, waiting for his own release. He did not relish the day when Elijah would leave him. Even as he thought of it, a vast, open space expanded in his heart. He knew he would feel an emptiness without his mentor. Truly, the Lord would need to be a very present companion in the absence of one who had filled his life with so much.

It was a lonely life, the life of a prophet. Many did not want to receive the words he brought them. But then there were also the rewarding times when God moved supernaturally on someone's behalf, supplying a need, healing a body. A myriad of experiences made him rely on the power of God more than any amount of intellectual knowledge he could muster. Yes, he would miss Elijah. He would feel most alone. This was the conversation Elisha had with himself several days before the Lord took his mentor. Without it being said, he knew it was time. But neither of them spoke of it.

He felt jolted into reality when those from the school of the prophets asked him, "Do you know that the Lord is going to take your master today?" Elisha didn't want to breathe a word of it, thinking that his silence would cause a delay. Elijah tried to ease the moment by excusing Elisha from his presence, thinking it kinder to spare his pupil the trauma of experiencing their separation first-hand. But Elisha would not hear of leaving him, remaining a stead-fast companion to the end. While the others watched them from a distance, choosing not to go the extra mile in favor of remaining where they were, Elisha pressed on. As Elijah struck the waters of the Jordan with his cloak, causing the river to part and allowing them to cross over on dry ground, Elisha marveled at the ease with which this great man of God operated in his calling. He walked in the assurance of God's presence and partnership. And he knew that this was the area in which he would be tried upon Elijah's departure.

This was an important time for Elisha. This would separate the principles of what he had learned from glaring reality. Now he would have to know and experience God for himself. With Elijah absent, would God still show Himself strong in their midst? This question beat in his heart so loudly he thought he could hear it in the air. He had to follow his teacher. He had to draw on him one last time. He needed what Elijah had to go the rest of the way alone. And so he summoned his courage when Elijah turned to ask him, "What can I do for you before I am taken from you?" Elisha imme-diately responded, "Let me inherit a double portion of your spirit." He hoped that Elijah would not consider this too bold a request. But the old prophet actually had a glint of admiration in his eyes when he replied that if his dear pupil saw him when he was taken from him, he could have the anointing. If this was some sort of way to test Elisha's depth of commitment and discipline, he would surely pass, so desperate was he for the fullness of God's power in his life. So keeping his gaze locked on Elijah, they continued on their way.

Suddenly a horsedrawn chariot of fire separated them, and Elijah was caught up in a whirlwind. Elisha stood down below beholding it all. He tore his clothes in respectful mourning, but inwardly he rejoiced at the way in which Elijah had been taken. It was a pronounced period at the end of the most incredible sentence one could write to testify of a life surrounded by God. With a sense of reverence Elisha picked up Elijah's cloak that had fallen amidst the awesome activity, and he returned in the direction from whence he had come. When he reached the Jordan he held his breath and hesitated for a fleeting second before striking the waters. Would the same God who had been with Elijah now be with him? He would soon find out. As the waters parted, Elisha felt a burden lift from his soul. God was his friend too!

It is easy for us to become spiritually intimidated when we're in the company of people who seemingly have it all together with God. Whatever our own relationship with the Heavenly Father, the sense of power emanating from those people cause us to question our own qualification to call God "friend." Our list of spiritual adventures is not as sensational as theirs, so when we really need a prayer to get through we know who to call because we know that God listens to them. But then one day they are no longer there and we have to call on Abba Father for ourself. With trembling hands we reach upward, not quite knowing what to expect. At times like this we must remember that there is only one true advocate who can sweet-talk God on our behalf. His name is Jesus. Based on our relationship with Him, and His relationship with the Father, God will move the heavens and the earth on our behalf.

Dear Heavenly Father, I feel as though I never pray enough, I never study Your Word enough, I don't know You as deeply as I ought to. Because of this spiritual handicap, I struggle with my faith though I long to have You show Yourself strong on my behalf. Please keep Your promise to me that as I draw closer to You, You will draw closer to me. Keep me ever aware that You do not compare Your children but meet them all individually where they live. I pray that I will not stay in the same place with You but will grow ever deeper, climb ever higher, and draw ever closer to Your throne. Allow me to see Your glory and Your manifest presence at work in my life. In Jesus' name, amen.

Who are the people in your life that provoke you to spiritual jealousy? What traits do they possess that you admire? What disciplines do you think they have instituted in order to reap the results you see? What steps do you need to take to reach your goals? Make a list for yourself and get to work.

THE INTIMIDATING TIMES

*When the servant of the man of God was risen early,
and gone forth, behold, an host compassed the
city both with horses and chariots. And his servant
said unto him, Alas, my master! how shall we do?*

2 KINGS 6:15 KJV

Why isn't Elisha worried? his servant wondered. *Doesn't he know this danger is too close for comfort?* This was an entirely different situation from helping needy widows or curing one of leprosy. They were surrounded by a hostile army and there was no escape! No one could come to their aid; they were hopelessly trapped. But this news did not seem to phase Elisha in the least. He simply knelt to pray, not for God to help them but for his own eyes to be opened. He had to admit that he was missing something he needed to see because from where he stood what he saw was not good. The troops of Aram were upon them.

Serving Elisha was always an adventure, but this was a little too much excitement for his servant's blood. It was one thing to be working on behalf of Israel. Then he was assured of God's interest. But was God really concerned with their personal safety? They were only two men, and he was even more insignificant than his master. Yet the answer to his questions was quickly made clear, for God opened his eyes to see the hillside around them filled with horses and chariots of fire. He was humbled by the reality of God's divine protection.

And then his master prayed another prayer: "Lord, please make them blind." And again the Lord did as Elisha asked. *Who is this God?* the servant wondered to himself as he walked with Elisha, leading this blinded army away from their doorstep and into the hands of the king of Israel. And how could He take such a personal interest in each person, no matter how great or small? This holy God, whose glory was so awesome that it had moved some to terror, would in the same breath rise to defend His own. This revelation rang in his spirit and resounded in his heart. How could anyone serve idols made of wood and stone when this living, breathing God was alive and willing to shed compassion and covering on all who worshiped Him? Of all that he had experienced while serving Elisha, this knowledge was his most precious treasure. God was interested in him, little ol' him! Let the enemy come; God would meet them. And no weapon that the enemy forged against Him would prosper.

When we walk only by what our human eyes see, we miss a greater opportunity to witness what the Spirit is able to reveal by divine insight. No matter how we feel or what we experience, God is always present. Quick to defend and protect His own, He will never leave us or forsake us. This has been a constant witness in my life when I have been assaulted by jealousy or the misunderstanding of others. As He causes our righteousness to shine forth as the noonday sun, His favor goes before us to bring us to a safe haven that is out of harm's reach or the enemy's tactics for destruction. And yes, He *is* interested in little ol' you!

Dear Heavenly Father, when fear and the threats of the enemy are all that I can see, open my eyes to see Your protection. Help me to rest in the knowledge that You are ever present, always loving, always covering me. You are my fortress and my hiding place. I rest secure within the strong tower of Your countenance. Continue to light my path with Your direction. Dispel my anxieties and build my confidence in Your promises toward me. Destroy the plan of the wicked against me; arise, O Lord, and let my enemies be scattered and all their advances against me be dissipated. Help me to remember that the battle belongs to You as I stand expecting Your salvation. Surround me with Your hedge of protection. Keep me ever in the circle of Your divine and blessed care. In Jesus' name, amen.

When threatened emotionally, physically, or spiritually, what is your first reaction? What former disappointments at the hands of other people have colored your perception of God's faithfulness toward you? Find scriptures that help you separate God's sovereign faithfulness from the fickleness of human devotion. Write a confession of God's promise to keep you in all your ways.

Still there is a place called alone that I seek
tucked beneath the arm of God
warm and sweet
A place where I can lay my weariness
and unanswerable questions
finding revelation in the rest
that His heartbeat gives
as I burrow deeper into the folds of
His breast
Lost in the depths of His mysteries
and riches untold
Found in His love
that always finds me
when I feel most alone
It is here that I find that the alone place
is no more than my own personal winter
where all that is in me dies
A season of the soul
pressed between the tendency
of my flesh and my heart to measure time
give it walls that hem in my spirit
and torment my faith
And so I wait for spring
and the warmth of the Son
to release me
from the coldness of fear
I throw my arms open surrendering to the light
until I find myself
basking in Your love
Reveling in the alone times....

THE REBUILDING TIMES

I went to Jerusalem, and after staying there
three days I set out during the night with a few
others. I had not told anyone what my God had
put in my heart to do for Jerusalem. There were no
mounts with me except the one I was riding on.

NEHEMIAH 2:11-12

Scanning the rubble, Nehemiah shook his head in dismay. Was he the only one who felt an overwhelming sense of pain looking at the wall in such a state of wreckage? Was this his burden and his burden alone? Had no one who had been living in Jerusalem been a little upset by this sight? He could no longer dwell on this; he only knew of one way to get rid of a burden, and that was to do something about it. If the desire to rebuild the wall was truly a nudge from God, He was well able to make provision for the task. This He had already proven. The king of Persia had been most generous to release Nehemiah from his post of serving him in order to let him begin this project. He had even contributed timber for the gates to the city and a cavalry to escort Nehemiah back in safety. This was much to the chagrin of the Israelites' enemies.

Yes, Nehemiah had come this far knowing that even to be standing in the midst of the wreckage was a miracle. He had been one of the exiles in Persia. He had felt the loneliness of being a stranger in a foreign land. Of struggling to deal with different languages, a different culture, even different gods. This is where he had felt most isolated. He clung to Yahweh with a fervency that many others hadn't managed to maintain. Thus, their captivity was the consequence. Yet God had remained faithful to Nehemiah throughout his stay, for God had crowned him with favor even in the midst of his captivity. And Nehemiah, for his part, had never let go of God's hand. He walked with Him. He talked with Him. He counseled with Him on every decision, every step of the way. And God was always there with the answer. As cupbearer to the king, Nehemiah was highly trusted—again, the providential hand of God at work. So when the exodus of the exiles back to Jerusalem began, Nehemiah, knowing he had not been put in such a prized position for nothing, stayed behind to wait on the voice of God for direction.

A visit from Nehemiah's brother bearing news of home was bittersweet. The joy of seeing his sibling was overshadowed by his report that those who survived the exile were back in the province deeply troubled and disgraced. The wall of Jerusalem had been broken down and its gates burned with fire. This so grieved the heart of Nehemiah that all he could do was weep. This was beyond distressing. How could he bear the weight of it? Then again, he was but one man. Those who had returned had not received the burden to do anything about this situation, yet he felt his heart would burst if things were not made right. He set his face to fast and pray before God, putting Him in remembrance of His word concerning the care of His people. He, Nehemiah, was willing to do his part to repair the broken places. But he couldn't do it alone. If God would be his ally, he would go.

The next day, King Artaxerxes noticed the forlorn countenance of Nehemiah and inquired about it. Once again Nehemiah breathed a prayer to God, asking for the right words to say. He then voiced his concern about the condition of his homeland, and the king asked Nehemiah his desire. This was his cue. "All right, Lord, here we go." He asked for the king's permission to go and rebuild the wall. His prayer was answered when the king consented. In the midst of opposition without and within, Nehemiah began a great work and refused to come down until it was finished. Unwavering in the face of threats, apathy, fearfulness, corruption, greed, and selfishness, Nehemiah refused to listen to any voice other than God's, and that one voice led him to the place of victory. It was a good work, and a good work always commands that God be glorified. And so it was that even their enemies were forced to accept the fact that this nation was not forsaken by its God. For only by the help of God had this work been completed.

A cause burns in our soul, and we ask ourself, *Doesn't anyone else see this great need as glaringly as I see it?* And then we find that God has allowed this vexation to spur us to rise to the occasion because, from the beginning, this was our God-ordained task. *But I feel ill-equipped to tackle this situation!* we think to ourselves. And God answers, "In and of yourself you are, but with My help nothing will be impossible to you." As we put our hand in His, He goes before us with His favor and provision. The Holy Spirit brings up the rear, saying, "This is the way; walk ye in it." And Jesus continues to intercede on our behalf and grant us the authority to step out in faith. Gazing in amazement at the accomplishment of what seemed to be an insurmountable task, we pause to give thanks, only long enough to receive the next phase of God's vision...but by this time we're ready.

Dear Heavenly Father, in my quest to find my purpose,
I am overwhelmed at how limited I am in my own

humanness. I long to do so much, and yet I feel so ill-equipped. And You come to me lovingly, reminding me that in my weakness Your strength is perfected in me. That You surpass my limitations in Your omniscience. And so I hold out my hands and yield them to You, right now. Holy Spirit, I yield to Your direction. Jesus, I rely on the strength of Your blood and Your authority to complete the work You've put before me. Help me to rest in the knowledge that what You commission, You also make provision for. In Jesus' name, amen.

What situation in the world or in your community burdens your heart? Have you ever considered being a part of the solution? What would you need to do in order to have the confidence to become involved? How does God fit into the picture? Write a prayer to God concerning the things that you grieve over, and ask Him to show you what part you can play in doing "a good work" to the glory of His name.

IN THE HEART OF THE INNER JOURNEY

THE BROODING TIMES

In the beginning God created the heavens and the earth. The earth was formless and empty, and darkness covered the deep waters. And the Spirit of God was hovering over the surface of the waters.

GENESIS 1:1-2 NLT

God sighed. It was a sigh like no other, for it revealed the heart of this Omnipotent God. The Alpha and Omega. The Beginning and the End. The One who had always been because He had always existed within Himself desired companionship. Though the heavenly host was in constant attendance, something was missing. Lucifer had left a tremendous gap after he was banished from the heavens for his rebellion. And though it was God's decision that this worker of iniquity depart from His presence, it did not lessen the pain He felt of losing not only one He considered a "son of the morning," but also a third of the angelic host. The absence of their voices, their praise and worship, left a void in the heavenlies. And that space grew even more immense with time. Yes, God was lonely. Lonely for those who would worship Him in spirit and in truth. Though praises rang constantly in His throne room, something was lacking. A note was missing from the harmony being sounded. It had sounded before but now it was gone; its absence was felt.

Never again would He make anything like Lucifer. He had made him perfect in every way, the most beautiful of all the angels, so beautiful that he had grown haughty at his own reflection. No, this time He would create man. An even more awesome creation than anything He had made in the heavenlies because he would be formed in His own image! Reflecting His likeness. This man would walk in perfect fellowship with Him. Fearfully and wonderfully made, he would be one who was like Him, created to fellowship with Him intimately. No longer would God place one in charge of gathering the worship and praise unto Him. Each man would come bearing his own chorus of praise. And the man would have access to bring his praise before God personally.

He considered the risks involved, mapping out the compensation for every weakness that this man would have. He knew that His greatest desire would also call for His greatest sacrifice, but still it would be worth it. Worth it to reclaim that note, that missing note that resonated in His soul. Life as it presently existed was like an unfinished symphony, lacking the sound of intimate worship flowing from a willing heart and creating its own sweet perfume. Heavy like incense, lingering long after the last chord had been echoed. And so, as all of heaven held its breath, God set to work. First He prepared a place for him to live. Not being made from the same substance as those in heaven, man would not be able to survive up there. He must be made from his surroundings in order to subsist.

Pondering all these details, God gazed down at Earth. He looked past the sphere, now dark and void, to light years beyond, knowing all that would transpire once He chose to fill it with life. "Let there be light!" He said, and the lights went on, warming the face of the frozen ball, melting the ice that covered it. And God separated the waters from the earth, furnishing this paradise with all sorts of incredible living things. But He saved His best creation for last—man himself. God gazed at this perfect wonder lying so peacefully still, one with the ground from which he was made. Ever so tenderly, He bent down and breathed into him the breath of life. Man became a living soul.

What pleasure this creation brought to God's heart! He anticipated their conversations in the cool of the evening. They were friends, exchanging freely. And yet He knew He could not keep Adam all to Himself. To do this would be to deny His own nature, which demanded that He give—because that's what love does. It was not good for Adam to be alone, as it had not been good for God Himself to be filled with such longing for the heart of another. So He fashioned for man an extension of himself, which He called woman.

But then one day the wonderfulness was marred. The moment it happened, the heavens reverberated from the cold air of separation that suddenly cut like a knife through the stratosphere. A note went sour in the midst of the chorus and God rose up to go down and see what had taken place for Himself. Keeping His usual evening appointment with the man and the woman, He found the garden strangely silent. And in His knowing He grew deeply sad. It had begun. The saga of all that He had foreseen had started. With this knowledge He made a sacrifice to cover their shame. He ached at the thought of the consequences their actions invoked because, in spite of their disobedience, He still loved them, still longed for their fellowship and worship. As He watched them leave the garden, He was already longing for the day when they would be able to return once again.

We have all experienced loving someone who offended us either consciously or unconsciously. Someone who chose not to love us back. We've felt the pain of separation and longed for restoration. It seems that, in their absence, the memories of our times together are magnified, leaving an even greater feeling of longing. This should give us an indication of how God longs after us. How wonderful to be able to rest in the fact that we can release all we are to Him and never, ever suffer from rejection. We love Him because He first loved us. We didn't choose Him; He chose us! He is so determined to embrace us that He promises that nothing shall ever separate us from His love. He calls us to be reconciled to Him through the shed blood of His Son, Jesus Christ. Through the blood we find our way back to the garden where we once again can stand before God, naked and unashamed.

Dear Heavenly Father, I come to You seeking total restoration with You. Today I would like to reestablish a love covenant between us. I ask that You take my filthy garments and wash them white as snow. I want to stand before You completely whole and unashamed, free to share all that I am with You. Thank You for first loving me. Thank You for giving Your Son just for me. Teach me how to walk in a way that is pleasing to You. Show me how to worship You in spirit and in truth, that I might fulfill my purpose and bring pleasure to Your heart. As I seek to draw closer to You, meet me and unfold Your nature and Your ways to me that I might grow ever more intimate with You as I increase in the knowledge of who You are. In Jesus' name, amen.

If you could walk and talk with God in the garden like Adam did, what questions would you ask Him? Why not make a date to meet and talk with Him? Make a list of the things in your heart that you've never really broached in prayer and lay them before Him. Then wait in His presence for an answer. Write down scripture references and phrases that begin to well up in your spirit as you wait in His presence.

_____

_____

_____

_____

_____

THE REJECTED TIMES

*Thereafter, Hagar used another name to
refer to the Lord, who had spoken to her. She
said, "You are the God who sees me." She also
said, "Have I truly seen the One who sees me?"*

GENESIS 16:13 NLT

What was she to do now? This was a fine mess she had gotten herself into. And yet Hagar found it hard to absorb the blame for all that had transpired. She had been minding her own business doing her maidly duties. It was Sarah who had suggested that her master Abraham sleep with her. Hagar had not volunteered for this attention. But Sarah, who had grown weary of waiting for the Lord to open her womb, had chosen her maid to be a surrogate mother and produce an heir for Abraham. And so she had complied.

The change in Sarah was immediate upon learning of Hagar's pregnancy. Sarah accused her of being contemptuous toward her. This was simply not true in Hagar's mind. She merely wanted to be treated with a little respect. After all, she *was* bearing Abraham's child. A bit of deference was the least she deserved! She must admit that she did feel a strange rush of power, and it expanded as the child grew within her. How fortunate she was. Who would have ever thought that this little Egyptian maidservant would end up bearing the heir apparent to this wealthy man? Truly the gods had smiled on her, or perhaps it was Abraham's God. She wasn't sure, for she wasn't acquainted with Him. She couldn't help it if

Sarah chose to feel insecure. That wasn't her problem. Like it or not, Hagar was the one with the child. Sarah would just have to deal with it.

But that was not the way it went at all. Sarah had grown increasingly harsh with her maid, and Abraham did not intervene at all. As Hagar's body went through the changes of pregnancy and her emotions ran the gamut as her system adjusted to the new life inside of her, the caustic barbs of her mistress made life unbearable. Perhaps this had not been a blessing after all, but a curse. How could she live in the midst of such immense jealousy and resentment? Why wouldn't Abraham come to her defense? And would her child also be subject to such cruel treatment? That was the last straw; Hager would never allow that to happen. And with that she ran away. Away from the constant bickering. Away from Abraham's weariness and weak apologies on behalf of his wife. Away from what she was certain would become a difficult environment for her child.

As she rested beside a desert spring along the road to Shur, trying to decide exactly which direction she desired to travel, an angel of the Lord approached her. He gently questioned what purpose she had for being in this place, and she replied that she was running away from her mistress. Surely the angel would see her side of the story. But instead he gently corrected her, telling her that she should return to her mistress and submit to her. Along with the correction came an incredible promise—she would have more descendants than she could count. She would give birth to a son and name him Ishmael, for the Lord had heard about her misery. The Lord had heard about her misery! This God who she had not acknowledged, knowing little to nothing about Him, cared enough to acknowledge her state of being, the bitterness of her soul!

Somehow knowing that God saw and cared made her able to deal with her circumstance. Yes, she would return to her mistress.

She would submit, come what may. She could endure Sarah's cutting remarks and rough treatment, for God had seen her misery. He had made her a personal promise. She would not look for a reward from Abraham or any other man. Her reward would come from God. "He is the One who sees me." These words rang in her heart all the way back home. They rang in her heart every time Sarah tried to ruffle her feathers and remind her of her subordinate stature. They rang in her spirit as she delivered her son, Ishmael, "God Hears." As she looked into the beautiful face of her newborn son, she saw the future promises of God in his eyes. Truly He had seen Hagar and heard the cry of her heart. This was beyond her expectations. This became the most humbling gift of all.

We all have a tendency to go on a power trip from time to time, getting a little too big for our britches or enjoying a bit of one-upsmanship when a situation turns in our favor in the presence of someone who previously bested us. But we need to be careful about doing this. Whether the one in authority over us is right or wrong, we must still remain in a place of submission. Because the more we rebel, the more the one in charge will tighten the screws on us. At that point we've become so focused on their attitude that we don't deal with our own. We wonder why God won't come to our defense and deal with this mean person who is bent on making our life difficult. Then, as we stop to catch our breath from the exertion of all our effort, God reminds us that we must first be obedient to His Word; He will take care of the rest. As we work as unto Him, in a stance of submission, He will bless us. He has seen our misery, He has heard our cry, and He has a promise for us that will make up for all that we have been through. But first we must return to Him and yield to His instruction.

> *Dear Heavenly Father, I confess my wrong attitude to You. I lay my rebellious heart before You and ask that You give me a clean heart and renew a right spirit within me. Help me to look past the present circumstance to see Your promises. Help me to hear beyond the remarks that cut, wound, and discourage. I want to hear the real need in the lives of those that You've placed over me in authority. As I walk softly before them, working as unto You, regard my situation and let not my enemies triumph over me. Lift me up and wrap me in Your peace. Let Your peace be my peace as I keep my eyes on You, knowing that You see and hear all. I know that You care for me and in this knowledge I will wait for Your redemption. In Jesus' name, amen.*

What have you been suffering through in your workplace? At home? In your church? At school? What have you contributed toward the problem? Confess these things to God and ask for His direction. Write a commitment to yourself and to the Lord detailing how you will proceed to handle your situation in accordance with His Word.

The valley and my heart are one
as I search for love
deep and unending
I find no stair to climb
my feet are soaked
from the rain of my tears
as I stroll through my longings
becoming drenched
in the rejection of others
and You come
gently covering me as I begin
to sink in the mire of my loneliness
You come replacing all that was before
folding me inside Your heart
carrying me to the mountaintop
where I see light
at the end of my desires....

THE SHAMEFUL TIMES

*Then Miriam and Aaron spoke against Moses because
of the Ethiopian woman whom he had married.*

NUMBERS 12:1 NKJV

Moses' wife watched the rumors circulate back to her husband, and she felt his pain. She hated being the source of contention; never did she want to cause any problems for him. Yet she didn't understand these people. She had never seen such murmuring and complaining among her own. She felt so blessed to be married to Moses. He was so kind. So humble. He was a good man, ruling fairly even when the people chose to be difficult. She had seen him crying out to God, and she had seen God answer him faithfully. She had chosen to embrace her husband's God after witnessing all of the marvelous miracles He had done for His people. But now she felt sad. She was an outsider. She was not one of them, and they made sure she and Moses knew it. Their words were hurtful. They questioned the leadership of Moses because of his wife, and she felt it was most unfair.

Within her she felt a nagging restlessness. *What is the deeper issue?* she wondered. Were they jealous of Moses' relationship with God, and, finding no fault in his leadership, had resorted simply playing up the one thing they considered a blemish in his life? As their prejudice rose to the surface she wondered with amazement how this could happen. They of all people knew what it was like to be oppressed and rejected because of their race, didn't they? She herself had not experienced slavery; she was a free woman who simply loved her husband and chose to leave her own culture to be with him. *How quickly we forget,* she thought. But this brought up a greater question. *They* were the ones with access to God. Aaron was a priest and Miriam a prophetess. If they felt this way about her, did God feel the same? Did He consider her an outsider because she was black? How could a God so great be so small if this were the case?

But Moses' wife soon found out that God's heart was very different from the hearts of Aaron and Miriam. God was not pleased with them. His anger burned against Aaron and Miriam as He rebuked them soundly. As He departed from them, Miriam was stricken with leprosy. Moses' wife found this rather ironic. How interesting that God would choose to give Miriam a taste of her own medicine! Miriam had judged someone on the basis of her skin, and now she must see how it felt to be separated and cast off because of what her skin looked like. Moses' wife watched Miriam in sympathy as she left the camp, no longer allowed to dwell within it because of her unclean condition. She knew how that felt, and she would never wish it upon others. Now Miriam would know too. Moses had told her that God had spit in the prophetess' face, so great was His distaste for her attitude. Moses' wife prayed for Miriam as they waited for her to return before they moved on. Because of the intercession of Moses, Miriam would only suffer from this condition for seven days.

Truly Miriam should appreciate God's kindness. Moses' wife chuckled to herself. Poor Miriam—she probably thought it an awful punishment to be a prisoner of her skin for seven days while she would remain different from the others all the days of her life. There was no simple solution for her. She would always encounter the ignorance and insensitive cruelty of others. But perhaps this was why she was so strong. She was bound to rely on the grace and favor of God in a world that would not always be kind. A world that was quick to judge and draw conclusions based on the color of one's skin. But on this day she was strangely comforted. God had spoken to her by His actions. He cared for her. He knew her pain intimately. He would be her advocate and her comforter, her defense and her strength.

It's true that people do not like what they do not understand. Fear presses strange buttons within all of us, from causing us to recoil from others for all the wrong reasons. We are reluctant to embrace anything different from the norm, yet God says that everything He creates is fearfully and wonderfully made. It's all good! He celebrates our uniqueness. He designed us in all shapes, sizes, and colors *on purpose*. He is a God of variety. He looks upon us all and sees an incredibly exquisite bouquet, one He was willing to pay an expensive price for. So when we choose to insult each other, God takes the insult personally. How dare one cause separation where He has decreed reconciliation! Reconciliation to one another and to Himself. Prejudice has no place in the kingdom. This grieves the Spirit of God, and it is not a matter that He allows to slide. He metes out judgment in the measure the offender serves up. But this is not where it ends. Even as the victims of offense grieve, God takes their pain to heart and draws close with empathetic arms to make His love and His presence known.

Dear Heavenly Father, I've been hurt by times when I have been the victim of other people's judgments and assumptions. It is painful—the cut is deep, and I find

it hard to forgive in these moments. I ask that You
insulate my heart and strengthen me that I might
always superimpose Your love over the cruelty of others.
Help my self-esteem not to be measured by what others
think of me, but rather by what You think of me. I
pray that as I walk through this life, I will be secure
in You in the face of every encounter, and that my
foundation for love and self-acceptance will be grounded
in You and Your proclamation over Your creation. I
am fearfully and wonderfully made, deliberately
crafted by Your hand to be exactly what and who I
am, and "it is good." In Jesus' name I pray, amen.

When you look in the mirror, what do you see? How do you feel about yourself? What would you like to change? What about you makes you feel like a victim of circumstance? How do the opinions of others shape your opinion of yourself? Do you feel bound by those opinions? Write down what you believe God thinks about you, then meditate on it.

You are the friend that sticketh
closer than a brother,
lover,
father, or mother,
for when I want to reach out to You
I need look no further
than my own soul
where You dwell
rising at every invitation
to greet me...
I wonder why I ignore You so long
seeking You in the faces
and arms of others
when all along You've been
right here,
nearer than I thought
nearer than I ever dreamed....

THE UNAFFIRMED TIMES

But the people broke in and said to Saul, "Jonathan has won this great victory for Israel. Should he die? Far from it! As surely as the Lord lives, not one hair on his head will be touched, for God helped him do a great deed today." So the people rescued Jonathan, and he was not put to death.

1 SAMUEL 14:45 NLT

Jonathan could not believe his ears. Then again yes, he could—his father, Saul, thought only of himself. He wondered if his father would ever learn the cost of moving by mindless impulse. He spoke without thinking, being careful only to protect himself at the cost of everyone else. Except now the "everyone else" was him. But that mattered not to Saul. His political career came before his children or even the warning of the prophets. He did his own thing, feigning deference to God but fooling no one in the process.

Now, out of ignorance, Jonathan had fallen into the line of his father's fire. Completely unaware of Saul's decree to kill anyone who ate food before evening—before he had avenged himself on his enemies—Jonathan scooped up some honey and ate it. He wondered why the others, who had the lackluster look of hunger and fatigue on their countenances, didn't do likewise. It was then that he heard of the decree, and it made no sense to him. How could hungry men fight effectively? Once again, because of his posturing, Saul had spoken to the detriment of his army. The men, exhausted after fighting the Philistines, fell upon the plunder too exhausted and famished to separate the blood from the meat. Someone pointed out that the men had fallen into sin in their haste to abate their appetites, and so Saul built an altar to the Lord to deter His anger. But was even this a sincere step on his part? No, he simply wanted to be free to return to the battle. The priests, however, recommended that they seek God before confronting the Philistines. This caused Saul great consternation. He was anxious to get on with the war. In haste he called for a lot to be drawn, swearing that if the sin that held them back from victory was upon even his son Jonathan, then he must die. He was willing to sacrifice even his own son for his selfish gain!

Jonathan, against his greater knowledge, still hoped there was something in his father that would click into good sense. Saul, though, was too far down the road to turn back now. It would be too much for him to admit that he was wrong. He had to go through with his decree to save face. Far be it from him to gain the reputation of a pushover, and so he stood his ground. He said it; he must now go through with it. But the men grew indignant. For once they could not go along with Saul's impulsiveness. They thought of themselves. If the life of his own son meant so little to the king, what was the value of their own lives? They were disturbed as they thought of their leader in this context. It was only a matter of time before their lives would be sacrificed without a second thought.

The pattern had grown too familiar, and now it was time to break it. So the men rose to Jonathan's defense. They defied Saul's orders, reasoning with him that it was Jonathan who had led them to victory; was this to be his reward? If so, they would have no part in it. How could they take the life of one who had saved their own? At this Saul, forever swayed by the opinion of others, relented. But something inside of Jonathan broke that day and left a void that only God could fill. The tie that binds father and son together had been severed by the cutting words of the father's foolish vow.

That his father would sacrifice his son to save face was the worst kind of affront. Jonathan always thought that a father was supposed to make sacrifices for the sake of his children. At least, this was *his* definition of love. But Saul loved only himself. Therefore Jonathan would turn his eyes upon God and give his heart to One more deserving. To One who thought it not robbery to sacrifice for Him.

The human frailties of our earthly parents can prove to be disappointing from time to time. Unfortunately, they can also do a lot to form our opinions of ourselves and shape our character. Jonathan knew his father had serious flaws, yet he tried his best to honor him in spite of them. This was not always easy. Eventually his close friendship with David gave him the bonding experience he never felt with Saul. David understood relationships and proved to be a steadfast friend. This was an extension of the relationship he had with God. Perhaps David shared with Jonathan what I would like to share with you now. While earthly parents can disappoint, we have a Heavenly Parent who never disappoints us. He is altogether lovely and perfect in every way. No dysfunctions here! When others give us distorted visions of who we are, He is there to affirm us and reveal who He created us to be—fearfully and wonderfully made, totally special, utterly loved and treasured. As a matter of fact, He loves us so much that He sacrificed His Only Son for us. Not out of foolish impulse. Not out of selfishness. But out of complete selflessness for our sakes. His sacrifice was made to forge a bond between us and Him that no outside force could ever sever. Nothing can separate us from His love.

Dear Heavenly Father, though I realize that human beings are not perfect, something inside of me expects more from my parents than they are able to give. Their failure to live up to my expectations and fill all of my needs leaves me wounded at times. I struggle often with my own identity in light of this. Even though they are there for me physically, I sometimes feel a deep sense of abandonment within. It is a void that creates great pain. I ask that You come and fill those empty places. That You be my Abba Father. That You pour out the love of a Father on me and heal the scars on my heart and in my mind. That Your presence be my affirmation. I choose to hide myself in You under the protection of Your wings, and rest in Your parentage. In Jesus' name, amen.

In what ways have your parents disappointed you? What things from their own experiences keep them from being free to be what you need? Was someone there for them in the capacity that you need them to be for you? Where does God fit in the midst of your expectations? What steps can you take to forgive your parents and free yourself to love them in spite of their failings? Write a list of the needs you perceive in them and ask God to show you how to minister to them in a way that would secure your own healing.

THE MADDENING TIMES

After this time had passed, I, Nebuchadnezzar,
looked up to heaven. My sanity returned, and
I praised and worshiped the Most High and
honored the one who lives forever.

DANIEL 4:34 NLT

Ah, this is the life…" Nebuchadnezzar stretched beneath the finery of his robes, feeling the silk caress his skin as the breeze atop his palatial rooftop perch cooled his bronzed cheeks. Yes, this was the life, and he had created it with his own hands. As far as the eye could see—as a matter of fact, even that which you couldn't see—it all belonged to him. What treasures he had accumulated! Among his favorites were the gold and silver vessels taken from the temple in Jerusalem. And then there was the majestic gold statue he had created. He frowned slightly as he recalled the controversy that had ensued after those three Hebrew boys refused to bow and worship it. They did indeed serve a powerful God. Why, after he had them thrown into the fiery furnace as punishment for their obstinance, this same God had descended from the heavenlies to walk in the midst of the flames with them. He had not even allowed the smell of smoke to penetrate their garments! No wonder they were so passionate in their allegiance to Him.

But none of the gods that Nebuchadnezzar acknowledged had ever displayed this same sort of intimate relationship with their worshipers, so he chose to remain cerebral in his approach to this "religion thing." He decided that if you didn't mess with the gods, they didn't mess with you. But what of the God of Daniel, Shadrach, Meshach, and Abednego? He had shown Himself mighty on their behalf, and the king had been forced to acknowledge His greatness. But what if it was all smoke and lights? Nebuchadnezzar knew that the magicians and sorcerers in his own court were capable of performing absolutely amazing tricks that could easily persuade one to conclude that they were assisted by a fearsome and mysterious god. Oh, well, whatever worked for them. As for himself, he believed firmly that the gods help those who help themselves. And he had helped himself rather well. He had built this kingdom with his own sweat and tears, his own brilliant military strategies, his own dreams—without any supernatural intervention.

And so Nebuchadnezzar ignored Daniel's warning of what would happen if he didn't acknowledge that "the Most High rules over the kingdoms of the world and gives them to anyone He chooses." The king chose to cling to his own personal brand of belief, the one that made him now sigh with great satisfaction as he surveyed the expanse of territory he reigned over. "Just look at this great city of Babylon!" he boasted. "I, *by my own mighty power,* have built this beautiful city as my royal residence and as an expression of *my* royal splendor." And on that note, he teetered on the brink of God's displeasure, then fell into the abyss of the deepest darkness a mortal could experience. For God had resisted his pride and removed the mantle of His favor, and there was nothing left once He withdrew. Not even the ability to maintain a sound mind. And so this great and powerful "self-made" king was reduced to wandering alone…driven from human society, living in the fields with the wild animals, eating grass like a common cow for seven years until something in his inner man broke and he yielded to the knowledge that, yes, there was One greater than himself…One who gave the power to gain wealth.

We, too, become drunk with our own sense of power. We develop convenient amnesia about the grace and giftings of God. We prefer to laud what we perceive as our own accomplishments won by our own efforts. But this thinking is madness. How, then, could we explain two people of equal intelligence and talents leading two very different existences? One of prosperity, one of mediocrity. Or one who is unqualified being exalted? The deciding factor becomes not the ingenuity of men, but solely the favor of God. Favor is merely One superior bending in the direction of one who is knowingly inferior. Without the favor of God, we are left to wander alone in the dark, in the wilderness of our own lack of understanding—keeping company with those who are no more than animals, free of a conscience that fears God, eating grass, experiencing that which is lower than what God intended for our spirit's consumption, preferring the counsel of the ungodly over the King's bread. The King's bread, God's Word, is the source of our life. And we, like Nebuchadnezzar, inevitably deteriorate—spiritually, physically, and emotionally—until we come to our senses and realize that pride is a lonely country that harbors no desirable citizens.

And so Nebuchadnezzar looked up to heaven. His sanity returned, and he praised and worshiped the Most High and honored the One who lives forever. And when his sanity returned, so did his honor and glory and kingdom. He was reestablished as head of his domain with even greater honor than before. But not before he learned one extremely vital lesson: It is a dangerous thing to praise yourself and ignore the One who made you. God refuses to share His glory with another—and that includes you. It is only when we truly make Jesus Lord of our lives that He makes us lord over all that lies within our reach, and even more.

*Dear Heavenly Father, in a world where we are
programmed to make things happen, help me to always
remember that You are the true author of days and
accomplishments. Help me to walk circumspectly before You,
redeeming the time, recognizing every season, never leaning
to my own understanding, but totally trusting in You. Help
me, in the midst of every victory, to seek Your purpose and
agenda. Help me to work with diligence, always knowing
that You are the start and end of all that I do. Let me never
presume to share Your glory. But rather let men see my good
works and glorify You in heaven. But most of all, dear
God, Abba Father, let me bring a smile to Your heart as I
lay all of my trophies before You. In Jesus' name, amen.*

What rewards or accolades have you taken for yourself? What
would you like to surrender to God right now in recognition of
His favor being manifested in your life?

THE WRENCHING TIMES

Then the LORD said to me, "Go and love your wife again,
even though she commits adultery with another lover."

HOSEA 3:1 NLT

Hosea knew what they were saying as he walked down the street, his head hung low in pain. Their conversations bore into his back along with their eyes. Some cast glances of pity, others of incredulity that he could be such a fool. Some were obviously past the point of sympathy, so great was their disgust that he would allow his wife to continue to behave in the way that she did. *Why should Hosea put up with Gomer's adulterous ways?* they wondered. Surely the law gave him compensation for a wife who insisted upon being wayward. But though Hosea knew all of this, he persisted in his love for Gomer.

The people shook their heads and wagged their tongues, watching him run after her as she left him time and time again to follow her lovers. And when her suitors were cold and cruel to her, stripping her of all she had, Hosea would faithfully make sure that Gomer had sufficient food and drink. He even provided her with linen and jewelry, which she took and either offered to Baal or shared with her various men. How much of an imbecile could Hosea be? Even the parentage of the children she bore was in question. How could Hosea be sure they were his own in the midst of her wanderings? She only returned when she came to herself and realized she would be better off with Hosea. But this decision lasted only for a season before her spirit grew restless. Hosea could see the boredom and the wanderlust begin to fill her eyes. He would silently pray for her to remain with him, but he would return home after a day of business to find her gone once again. The rumor mill was always faithful to supply her location. And Hosea, knowing the man she was currently with had nothing to offer, would leave provisions for her and go his way patiently awaiting her return.

Yes, it was true Hosea's pain was great—but Hosea was a prophet. His life was a parable come to life that showed how God felt about the children of Israel. He was the faithful husband longing after his unfaithful wife. Always willing to forgive, to comfort and restore, regardless of the offense. And so Hosea continued on his trek to find Gomer and look after her welfare. He found her this time broken and in even deeper trouble than the last time he'd rescued her from one of her paramours. This time she had been sold into slavery. No one could believe that he would spend even one shekel to buy her back, yet that was exactly what he did. With fifteen shekels, a homer, and a lethek of barley, he bought her back and took her home, speaking tenderly to her all the way while she looked on with unappreciative eyes.

Hosea didn't mind doing this for his wife; he knew that everyone was given a season of grace before judgment would come. God would not forsake him and allow him to be abused forever. He would come with deliverance in His wings and restoration in His hands. Until then Hosea would wait on the Lord, allowing Him to renew his strength. For he had been party to the fellowship of God's suffering with His people. If anyone knew His heart at this point, it was Hosea. He knew the pain of separation and unfaithfulness and how, in spite of it all, love prevailed. It was strange to describe this thing called love or figure out exactly how it worked.

It was higher than he imagined, yet bent lower than he thought he would ever be able to go. And yet it expanded beyond the widest reaches of his soul, even when offended by the object of his affection. It was certainly larger than him, Hosea concluded, yet it included him completely in the circle of God's endless love. It was that love that freed Hosea to love the "unlovable."

What can separate us from the love of God? Our own foolishness? Mindless mistakes? Deceived hearts or distorted vision? No, nothing can stop Him from longing after us, from being willing to forgive us time and time again. This does not, however, separate us from the consequences of our sin. Nevertheless, He is there, ready to heal the sting that consequences bring until we finally learn that it is not profitable to stray. But in the meantime His agape love, that "in spite of yourself" love, covers a multitude of sins. Its wooing power takes us to another place of humble surrender. For who can resist a lover who gives all, even when we're not ready to receive? It's simply a matter of time before we find ourselves addicted to His goodness. Completely "soul'd" out, finding all other influences who come to woo us hopelessly inferior to Him.

Dear Heavenly Father, forgive me for the times I've strayed and gone in search of the other lovers of my soul. Forgive me for the times I gave in to those who courted my flesh and abused the deposit of Your Spirit within me. As I return to You, I pray that You will wash my heart and make my spirit new within me. Cast me not away from Your presence, my Lord and Savior. I, like

David, cry out, "Take not Your Holy Spirit from me."
Restore the joy of my salvation to assuage the sting of
sin. As You surround me once again with Your love, do
not allow the shouts of condemnation to drown out
Your tender voice. Speak to me and I will listen and
yield to what You say. Hedge me in round about and
keep me by Your side. And as I learn of Your bountiful
grace and mercy, help me to rest in Your peace, safe
within Your arms forevermore. In Jesus' name, amen.

What forms do the other lovers in your life take to draw you away from God? When do these diversions usually crop up in your life? Do you recognize a pattern that can give you a clue about how to protect your heart? Write the areas of weakness that leave you open for temptation. Find scriptures to combat the feelings that rise at these times. Write a new love commitment to the Lord, and enlist His help to keep it.

_____

_____

_____

_____

THE URGENT TIMES

*Just then a woman who had been subject to
bleeding for twelve years came up behind him
and touched the edge of his cloak. She said to
herself, "If I only touch his cloak, I will be healed."*

MATTHEW 9:20-21

She had nothing to lose, for everything had been lost already. She had spent all she had on physicians who offered a cure yet never delivered. Her health had been spent along with her money. Weak and anemic from bleeding for so many years, she saw this Jesus as her last resort. The stigma of being continually unclean was too much for her to bear. But on this day she had no concern for the jostling crowd and those who pressed against her; she was on a mission.

After all that she had heard concerning Jesus, she had purposed in her heart that she must get to Him. And so she had waited for His arrival. It was Jesus or nothing. Clasping her hope against her breast with bony fingers, she decided that perhaps she should not ask Him to touch her. She could not bear His refusal. It stood to reason that she was of small consequence in light of the more urgent matters of others. No, she wouldn't bother Him with her issue. If He was all that she had heard, she believed that there would be healing power even in His garments. She reasoned within herself that if what flowed from within her had the power to make anything she sat or lay upon unclean, and anyone who touched where she had been became unclean as well, then surely the virtue that flowed within this man was also on whatever He touched, including His clothing. "If I just touch His cloak, I will be made whole," she said to herself. If there was a penalty to pay, it would be worth it, so great was her longing to be made whole.

It was now or never—she instinctively knew this. So as the pressing of the crowd grew more insistent, she stretched forth her hand and touched the edge of His cloak. Time stood still in suspended animation. Strength began to course through her limbs, and she could feel the flow of blood stopping. She had been made whole! But her rejoicing was cut short as Jesus stopped abruptly. The crowd also stopped. His voice was magnified over the silence: "Who touched Me?" The people looked from one to the other, hunching their shoulders, looking vaguely perplexed. Touched Him? How could He not be touched in the middle of such a throng? Everyone was touching Him, but certainly not deliberately. They were not here to offend; they had come simply to see Him. To get a word, to get a touch as He willingly chose to do so. No, indeed, no one had touched Him on purpose. And why would this be an occurrence of note anyway? But He continued to insist that someone had touched Him. He had felt virtue leave His body. In that instant she knew that she was the culprit and that she dare not hide. She could not steal her healing. She only prayed that when she confessed, it would not be taken from her.

Pressing forward, head held low, knees trembling, she could no longer stand in His presence. Falling at His feet, she poured out her story to Him. Of the pain, the shame, the suffering she had endured. How she hadn't wanted to bother Him. But she was desperate. She just wanted to be well again. To be made whole. To have a normal life. Surely He could understand her distress and have pity….And then true healing came! He released her to go in peace, acknowledging her faith. "Her faith had made her whole,"

He said. Oh, if only she had believed sooner…but today was just as good a day to begin.

To accept the labels that life puts on us is to accept certain defeat. It is up to us to press through the crowd of doubts, fears, and untruths that keep us bound. Stretching forth and breaking through to the place where we reach Jesus and grab hold of His virtue must become our all-consuming mission. By exercising our arms of faith, we strengthen our whole body. We must stop allowing the enemy to drain us with negative confessions about ourselves. We are not doomed to forever live in defeat. We are not lost causes. We are desirable. We are lovable. We are wanted. We have all that we need within us because Jesus lives inside of us. In our weakness He is made strong. Let God arise within you. Let Him empower you to receive the healing—mental, spiritual, emotional, or physical—that is already yours to embrace.

Dear Heavenly Father, I realize that in and of myself I can do nothing and that I am nothing without You. I celebrate my nothingness, realizing that in this I leave room for You to be everything in me—all the strength I need. All the power I need. All the love I need. I am complete in You, for You are my sufficiency. Thank You for Your constant care and compassion. Thank You for meeting me where I am today. In the midst of all my fears and turmoil, make Yourself available for another touch. Another touch to renew my faith and rebuild the broken areas of my spirit. As I reach out to You, meet me with all that I need to overcome

*my present trials as well as those things that seek
to cling from my past. In Jesus' name, amen.*

What are the things that you feel hinder you from being whole? What issues seek to keep you separated from the One who can heal you? Locate the lies of the enemy that keep your faith from rising. Find a scripture to address your pain and doubt. Meditate on His Word to you and release the things that are keeping you bound.

_____

_____

_____

_____

_____

THE REMORSEFUL TIMES

Then Peter remembered the word Jesus had spoken:
"Before the rooster crows, you will disown me three
times." And he went outside and wept bitterly.

MATTHEW 26:75

What is it about my mouth? Peter wondered. It seemed to have a life all its own. It didn't matter what he intended to do in his heart; his mouth ignored his good intentions and took off on an entirely different course. *Why do I do that?* he wondered. He was invariably saying something he shouldn't say, and Jesus was continually rebuking him. It always seemed the right thing to say until the words came out of his mouth. They then turned sour and left a bitter feeling in the pit of his stomach. Peter remembered the countless times that Jesus had questioned the motive of his heart based on the things he had said. And each question magnified his lack of understanding concerning God's purposes in Jesus' life. Peter thought he got it, but he really didn't. He realized that now more than ever since Jesus had been arrested. He felt confused, thrown off balance, afraid, no—downright terrified. Everything had happened around him way too fast. He felt as if he were one pebble in the midst of a huge avalanche and he was forced either to roll in the rush down the mountain or be crushed. And so his mouth had once again spouted words in haste—words that never should have been spoken. Except this time the words were more offensive than any he had ever uttered before.

Jesus had told Peter that he would deny Him three times before the cock crowed. Peter had thought it quite insulting at the time. *How could He ever think I would do such a thing? Doesn't He know how much I love Him?* he had thought. Jesus' words had hurt him deeply. What did He take him for? And why have Peter around if He thought so little of him? He felt that he was being judged for his impulsiveness, which had become an obvious trait in Peter's life. He felt weary at the thought. Would he ever be able to live down his reputation for always saying the wrong thing at the wrong time? Well, this time he had really done it. He had denied Jesus—three times before the cock crowed, just like He said it would happen. But this time it was not just a matter of realizing he had said something he shouldn't have. Peter felt it sealed Jesus' fate in a strange sort of way. If this had come to pass, it meant that all the other things Jesus had said would come to pass too.

Why had he denied Jesus? Was it because he feared being recognized as the one who had cut off the soldier's ear in the garden? Was he afraid of being accused of treason against the Roman government and suffering some brutal punishment? What had happened to Peter's declarations of being willing to die with Jesus? Those had quickly gone out the window when his own skin was being threatened. What a wimp! And Jesus had known all along exactly what he had been made of. The truth hurt, and Peter wept bitterly. He wept over all the lost opportunities to do something that really counted. The conversations that were never truly appreciated. The words he never took to heart. The revelations he refused to embrace. The truth he refused to see. And now the time was gone. Jesus was gone. He would never have another chance to show Him how far he had come. And he had contributed to his beloved Teacher's demise. Why had Jesus ever called Peter to follow Him if He knew all of his weaknesses? What had He seen in him that was worth salvaging? And now that he'd blown it, where could he go to get away from himself and what he had done? Where could he go for forgiveness? For restoration?

Oh, would there be no end to his weeping and brokenness of heart? Days of emptiness passed while Peter rehearsed his regrets over and over again. And then Mary came, saying that Jesus had risen from the dead! Did he dare hope for another chance to make amends? But when Jesus appeared to him, He never addressed Peter's denial. Never accused or rebuked him for his weakness. He had moved beyond yesterday. His mind was on the future. "Peter, do you love Me?" What a question! Of course he loved Jesus! "Then feed My sheep," his Teacher answered. It was the least Peter could do. No longer did he feel any fear and trembling or false bravado. There was something he wanted more than the acceptance of men, something he never wanted to be separated from again—the love of his Lord. The impulsive little boy in Peter had died with Jesus on the cross, and a man had been resurrected with his Savior. Though he had denied Him in the face of a small cluster, he would now go to the ends of the world to proclaim the name of Jesus. Gone were his insecurities. Gone was his fear of repercussions or even of death. Peter knew now what he did not know before—nothing could separate him from God's love.

Our failings are cruel voices that accuse and demoralize us. They tell us that we are no longer worthy of God's love and attention. That we've messed up big time. That there is no redemption of our circumstance. Our self-worth plummets, and we begin to agree with our accuser that there is nothing good in us, nothing worth salvaging. And then Jesus comes with a new commission for our lives, heaping blessings on top of our incredulity that He still loves us in spite of our foolishness. He extends His grace to us for a new beginning and a better tomorrow, and we're made a little stronger and a whole lot wiser. Thank God for His mercy, for He knows we are but dust. Thank God that He is the God of as many chances as we need to get it right!

> *Dear Heavenly Father, I thank You. I thank You simply because You have chosen to love me. In spite of my failings and my flaws, You continue to extend Your mercy and grace to me. Without it I am nothing, but with it I am filled with the sufficiency of all that I need to become all that You would have me to be. I stand before You as a willing vessel longing to pour out to others all that You have deposited in me. Fill me with Your understanding and wisdom that I might walk in the Spirit and not be drawn away by the rationalizations of the flesh. Replace my fears with unshakable faith that I might forsake the opinions of man and strive to please only You. Fill me with a love and passion for You that overrides my appetite for anything that is not of You. Help me to exercise discipline and walk in agreement with You as You order my steps, my words, and my thoughts. Let all that I do be found acceptable in Your sight. In Jesus' name, amen.*

What are some of the past failings in your life that you have found difficult to get over? Have you moved past conviction to accepting condemnation on these issues? Are these continual habits or one-time offenses? What can you do in light of God's Word to get past the oppression that comes with residual guilt? Write a confession to God and put it under the blood once and for all. Ask Him to give you a new commission. Write a scripture verse of forgiveness that you can meditate on.

_____

_____

_____

_____

_____

Perhaps I thought
I had to reach too high
to get to You
who knows the excuse?
it always seems too easy
to simply find You
where You always are
waiting for me…
for who is man
that God should desire him
live for him
die for him?
and yet You've done just that
and I am ashamed of my own selfishness
my own insistence that You be complicated
giving me a reason to admire
my own spirituality
it is far too humbling to know
that all I have to do
is call Your name….

THE REACHING TIMES

He wanted to see who Jesus was, but because
he was short he could not see over the crowd.

LUKE 19:3

Ignoring those who glared openly at him as he passed by, Zacchaeus kept his eyes focused on the object of his concentration. He didn't care that they hated him. He didn't care that they resented his presence. He had one mission in mind—seeing this man who everyone was talking about. This Jesus. From his vantage point he strained to see Him. The crowd seemed to block his view on purpose, milling about their enigmatic guest. Not one to be put off easily, Zacchaeus determined to devise a way to see Him. Who was this Jesus? Another religious zealot who would incite the people not to pay their taxes? This could cause great problems for him. He had to scope this guy out—get a handle on him, and plan his next move accordingly. Yes, he must see this Jesus if it was the last thing he did. So let the people think whatever they wanted to think; their stares would not deter him.

Running ahead of the throng, Zacchaeus scoped out the scenery for the perfect spot. Aha! Perfect! This tree would serve as an excellent vantage point for him. So up he climbed, finding the perfect view on one of the lower branches. He could actually witness everything he needed to see and hear without being noticed, far removed from the press of the crowd. But all of a sudden Jesus looked up, straight into his eyes. He froze, not knowing what to expect. Would Jesus now resort to hurling accusations at him? He would be an easy target. Everyone hated him. He was wealthy, a tax collector, and they accused him of being a traitor and a cheat. Yes, he would be the perfect scapegoat if that's what Jesus needed to manipulate the crowd into seeing things His way. But instead Jesus did something entirely unexpected. He asked Zacchaeus to come down from his lofty seat and take Him to his house. Just think—this Jesus wanted to be his houseguest! Who would have thought it?

This did not set well with the crowd at all. Immediately a wave of disapproval swept through the gathering, but Jesus seemed oblivious as He focused on Zacchaeus. Zacchaeus, on the other hand, was so thrown off-balance by this strange invitation that he was initially taken aback. And then it hit him. Jesus was sincere! He really *did* want to get to know him. *Little ol' me,* Zacchaeus thought. *I am the one that everyone despises and yet their hero wants to spend time with me.* This had a strange effect on him. It was humbling to be sincerely reached out to. No one had extended this sort of kindness to him for as long as he could remember.

From the time he was a child, he had been ridiculed because of his small stature. Pushed and shoved. Teased and tormented. Many a tear of self-pity had been shed. Deep within his child-like heart Zacchaeus vowed that things would be notably different when he grew up. No one would push him around—he would be the one calling the shots. And those who made his life difficult would get a taste of their own medicine. He would show them all. And so he took advantage of the system instilled by the Romans and moved up the ranks to become a tax collector. He had not cared about the people who struggled to keep up with what they owed. He showed no mercy when demanding balances from his debtors. The taunts of the neighborhood children came back to haunt him, and those were enough to strengthen his resolve. He would not back down.

And now Jesus didn't care about his size. Didn't care that he was a tax collector. Didn't care that He would receive bad press because He chose to associate with Zacchaeus. Suddenly Zacchaeus felt important—not because of position, not because the Roman government said so or because the people said so. He felt important because *God* said so. As affirmation flooded his heart, his mind was changed, his countenance transformed. Suddenly he saw himself for what he had become. Saw how his striving to be over people had actually belittled him even beneath his diminutive stature. He wanted to be totally deserving of God's compassion. Though that could never be, he had to do something as a token of gratitude. It was interesting what a word from God could do. Suddenly all that he had hoarded in order to build himself up meant nothing. A word from God had made him full. "Look, Lord," he vowed, "here and now I give half of my possessions to the poor, and if I have cheated anybody out of anything, I will pay him back four times the amount." The relief he felt upon uttering this promise was like opening wellsprings deep within his soul. Joy washed over him like a waterfall. He was free! Free to be accepted! Free to be loved! Free to be embraced as a son of God! For the first time, Zacchaeus knew what it was like to truly stand tall.

Shortcomings truly do cause us to "act out," to overcompensate for the me we think we should be. Trying to measure up to the standards of others can be debilitating because we will undoubtedly fall short of their expectations. The beauty we can find in the midst of our own imagined failings is that God loves us just the way we are. He doesn't think we're too tall, too short, too fat, too thin, too dark, too light, too ugly, or too anything. He just sees His child struggling for affirmation, for the reassurance that we're all right. And based on our relationship with Him, He gently reminds us that we are fearfully and wonderfully made. Deliberately crafted just the way we are to be a unique member of His divine family. One that He welcomes with open arms because all of our imperfections become perfect in the light of His love.

Dear Heavenly Father, I apologize for the times I have looked in the mirror and failed to see what You see. I pray that my lack of appreciation has not been an insult to Your handiwork. Open my eyes to see my beauty in the light of Your love. Grant me an appreciation of the me that You've created and help me to give it all back to You for the fulfillment of Your purposes. I choose to walk in the beauty of holiness when my flesh tugs me toward the ugliness of sin. May my stature be measured by my righteousness and not by physical inches. Today I release the disappointment I have felt over what I feel I should have been and lay all that I am and all that I hope to be at Your feet. Renew my mind so that I may get a new vision of what is truly important. Take me and make me an instrument of Your love and power. In Jesus' name, amen.

What are the things about yourself that you don't like? How do you compensate for what you view to be your shortcomings? How do others perceive your actions? Write a list of the things that you don't like, then find corresponding scriptures based on what God thinks about you in that particular area. Memorize and apply God's perspective to your view of yourself.

_____

_____

_____

_____

_____

THE RESIGNING TIMES

"We had hoped that he was the one who was going to redeem Israel. And what is more, it is the third day since all this took place. In addition, some of our women amazed us. They went to the tomb early this morning but didn't find his body."

LUKE 24:21-23

Sadness hung like a heavy, wet blanket over the men as they walked. Completely lost in thought, they continued commiserating amongst themselves on the events of days gone by, unable to shake the disappointment and depression they felt at Jesus' departure from their midst. Jesus was gone. They had hoped that He was the Messiah, but once again their hopes had been dashed. And now He was gone. Even more perplexing, the women in the group had returned from His gravesite to say that His body was missing. Yes, some of the disciples swore that they had seen an angel, who told them that Jesus had risen from the dead. Yet how were they supposed to believe that? Considering the treachery of what had recently taken place, it seemed quite clear that His body had been stolen. Who would put it past those men who had been bent on causing trouble and stirring the masses against Jesus? Couldn't they have just granted Him the peace of leaving His body in the grave? Was that too much to ask? It was hard enough to absorb all that had occurred without this new and traumatic turn of events.

As they walked and talked, Jesus joined them. But so deep was their sorrow they did not recognize Him. The tears in their soul distorted their vision, and He became just another stranger to them. And then this stranger had the audacity to interrupt their conversation. He asked them what things had them so deeply concerned. What things? *What things!* Where had this man come from? Hadn't He heard any news of the last four days? He simply stood there, calmly taking them in, His face free from pain or worry while they were practically bowed over with their cares. Now they must stand and explain to this clueless stranger the things that grieved their very souls. And then He called them foolish! They didn't know if they should grow indignant or just ignore Him as He began to quote scripture after scripture of the prophets' predictions about the Messiah. Though they failed to see how this connected to what they had told Him, it comforted them in a strange way. And so they invited their new companion to remain with them for the evening.

As they sat to eat, they felt as if they were experiencing déjà vu. Their guest took the bread, broke it, and blessed it, and suddenly their eyes were open. But as soon as they recognized Him, He had vanished. *But of course!* they thought. They should have known! They recalled the way they had felt when He began to unfold the scriptures to them as they walked. How could they have been so blind? They must tell the others! They would not make the same mistake again if given another opportunity to see Him. By the time they reached the other disciples, Peter, too, had seen Him. It was all too much for them to take in. How could this be? Was He a figment of their imagination, perhaps their own wishful thinking had willed Him back to them in the form of a mirage? And then He was standing among them again. And they were afraid. As He ate the food they provided, He fed them with more heavenly fare—bread from the Word of God. Finally they understood all that He had tried to reveal to them before. What was formerly dead to them became alive in their hearts, and the truth rang in their spirits. This time as Jesus was taken away on a cloud into glory, His absence had an entirely different effect on His disciples. Instead of being defeated by depression, they were invigorated with joy. Despair was replaced by faith while loss was eradicated by restoration. They had a hope, a future, an expected end. And a profound message to share with the world!

"Every good-bye ain't gone," the old folks say. And it is true. The things that we think are dead in our lives miraculously return anew when the Lord breathes on them. As we bemoan the fate of lost dreams, lost loves, and lost opportunities, Jesus sidles up beside us. As we mourn the loss of what once filled us with hope or fulfillment, He asks us, "What things?" Sometimes in the depth of our despair, we also don't recognize His visitation. We spend far more time grieving than we ought to and miss the opportunity to rejoice with the One who has control over all "things" in our lives. When we finally get to the place where we understand that nothing is lost in Him, and that everything that is of God in our lives will always remain, life will become a more even road to travel. When we look to see Jesus walking beside us, then, and only then, will we be able to embrace the power and help He brings to restore all we feel we've lost.

Dear Heavenly Father, I take all that I've seemingly lost and all that I hope to gain and place them on Your altar. I know that it is not by might, not by power, but by Your Spirit that all things are gained. I know also that You are able to keep whatever is committed to You. So with that in mind, I commit all my dreams, hopes, desires, and longings into Your hands. Please keep them safe and deliver them up at the right time. I know that You know what is best for me and that You know the way I take. So I ask for the deliverance of Your perfect plan for me according to Your divine timetable. Help me to remember that nothing is lost in You and all that I am is found only in You. In Jesus' name, amen.

Make a list of your lost dreams, opportunities, and even loves, and give them all to God. As you sacrifice these things to Him, ask for His direction. Which things should you release? Which things should you trust Him to bring to pass in His perfect timing? Which things are good and perfect gifts and which things are distractions of the enemy to get you off-course? Settle all your questions with Him today, and choose a scripture you can rest on.

*And at the ninth hour
Jesus cried with a loud voice, saying,
Eloi, Eloi, lama sabachthani?
which is, being interpreted,
My God, my God,
why hast thou forsaken me?*

MARK 15:34

THE PRAYERFUL TIMES

*He took Peter and the two sons of Zebedee along with
him, and he began to be sorrowful and troubled. Then
he said to them, "My soul is overwhelmed with sorrow to
the point of death. Stay here and keep watch with me."*

MATTHEW 26:38

They couldn't stay awake and pray for Him even for just one hour. One little hour! How long had He been with them? Three years? Sometimes it felt like ninety, and yet it would now be over too soon. He loved His disciples. They were made up of the most interesting conglomeration of personalities and temperaments. There was Peter, who always had to have the last word in any given conversation. John, who loved Him. James, with his thunderous temper. He loved them all. They were good men—all twelve—sincere even when they were wrong. They gave their all; they put their faith in Him. At times that faith was a bit misplaced, but nevertheless they were steadfast. Needless to say, they had kept life interesting.

He gazed at them as they slept now, completely out of tune with what was about to occur. He thought of the others—Matthew, Mark, Philip...on and on His mind scanned through images of them in His head as if looking at them for the last time. He stopped at Judas. Poor Judas—he had opened himself up to be used as an instrument of the devil. How this deceived one would suffer after He was gone! Judas would never know that all was well, that Jesus had to die to save them all. He thought of the upcoming days and His eyes grew dark with pain. Pain for the agony He knew they would experience because of their continued lack of understanding. They would see soon enough. And then a greater pain washed over Him.

Though He had volunteered for the mission of giving His life so that the world through Him might be saved, the process would be a difficult one, like nothing He had ever before experienced. He literally would take on the sins of the world. He who knew no sin would become sin. But in the process He would be separated from the Father. He had never been separated from Him, and the thought of it was unbearable. It brought a violent shock to His system, so extreme that He sweated drops of blood as He prayed one last prayer for the disciples. For the world. For Himself. From the beginning it had been Him, His Father, and the Holy Ghost, so close that they were one. Extensions of each other. Literally beginning and ending one another's sentences. All that He was and all that He did revolved around the Father. He lived for Him. He breathed for Him. He had His very being in Him. Conversing with Him was like breathing. He couldn't bear the thought of having their fellowship broken. To not experience divine intimacy with Him was worse than anything He could imagine. He would rather experience anything but that. No matter how brief the time of their separation, it would seem an eternity. He would die a million deaths inside, though His body would only go through one.

But He was determined to complete what He had started. He only wished that there was another way. And then His attentions turned to the disciples and all of those He had taught. He prayed that the Father would keep them. They, too, would go through the bitterness of separation and much heartache. In this He had the advantage. He knew what was happening; they did not. They had yet to truly perceive the meaning of all that He had told them. Their confusion would be great, and He prayed that they would not scatter. But He also knew that the suffering they were about to encounter would produce perseverance and character. In light of this they would be strengthened to have immovable hope. Oh, He could see what these men would become once they endured this test. Fearless, mighty men of God. It made His present pain worthwhile.

He longed for the day when He would show them around heaven and they would see His glory. It was so far beyond their comprehension that He had not even tried to describe it to them. They only knew Him as He was with them on earth; they did not know another side of Him—the side where He sat among the host of heaven, exalted above every name. His garments gleamed and the holiness of God shone forth from Him like gold. The side where He was one with the Father. He wanted them to see and experience this, to have that same oneness. To be free from all that bound them on earth. This was His prayer and the expectancy that spurred Him toward the finish line. As He looked beyond the disciples down through the pages of time, He saw the names of the others who were written in the Lamb's Book of Life. All of those people He already knew would come to be a part of the Bride of Christ, joined forever with Him in eternity—you and I joyfully being among that number—and He also prayed for us! That we would be partakers of all that He was and have fellowship with the Father unbroken throughout eternity.

And then He rose to the occasion and went forth to meet His fate, strong in His resolve to have us all by His side forever. He was accused, abused, beaten, and crucified. As He became sin for us, God turned His face from Him, unable to bear the stench of sin in His nostrils. And then the moment Jesus most dreaded came to pass. His soul was ripped, His spirit shattered by the vast void of darkness as He felt the light of God removed from Him. How great a darkness it was! While others wondered at how quickly He died, commenting on how unusual it was, they failed to recognize that no cross could kill Him. Only separation from His Father could. He gave up His life rather than endure the torture of this state. But then on the third day He rose and ascended back to the Father. In parting from the disciples this one last time, He sympathized with their pain caused by the separation and promised them a Comforter, a deposit of Himself that would be with them until they met again. They must trust and know that they would never be alone.

We have all offended a loved one and felt the pain of separation. But how many of us despair over being separated from our Heavenly Father? As we move from fear to faith to love in our Christian experience, we are subject to different depths of emotions toward God. Most of us have an intellectual understanding of who God is and what Christ did for us, and we are quite content to keep our relationship with them at face value. We are grateful, acknowledging that we need what They have to offer, and we're content to leave it at that. But there is another place where a deeper and sweeter coexistence can take place. When we truly fall in love with Jesus, embrace our Abba Father, and walk in total dependence on the leading of the Holy Spirit, something happens. A powerful connection. A love connection. The fellowship and intimacy that comes out of that is addictive. So sweet, so rich, so all-consumingly satisfying, we will crave it always. And though many things assault us each and every day that threaten to separate us from our love source, the thought of separation becomes overwhelming. We find ourselves scurrying back to our rightful position, resuming the flow of intimacy. Reveling in His love for us. Never alone.

Dear Heavenly Father, thank You for all You have done for me. Thank You for loving me enough to give Yourself totally through Your Son, Jesus, to redeem me. Thank You for the interest You show in every little detail of my life, for sending me a Comforter to lead and guide me. But most of all I am overwhelmed by Your constant and faithful love. I simply ask You this: Fill me to overflowing with love for You. Let it seep out of every part of me and let everything I do be an outpouring of my adoration for You. I am not seeking a religious experience; I crave true relationship with You. I ask You to teach me the things that Jesus knew. Show me the secrets of how to have the same type of relationship that He had with You. I want to be a true son (or daughter), able to rest in the knowledge that You and I are one. Forever one. In Jesus' name, amen.

How important is your relationship with God to you? Do you crave to draw closer to Him? Do you feel the separation when you do not? What are the things in your life that are roadblocks to intimacy with Him? How can you begin to remove them? Write a love pact with the Lord. Tell Him what you need to draw you closer to Him.

About the Author

Michelle McKinney Hammond, bestselling author (whose books have sold more than 1.5 million copies), singer, and speaker, focuses on improving love-driven relationships. She's the founder and president of HeartWing Ministries and previously cohosted the Emmy Award-winning *Aspiring Women* for 10 years and TCT's *3D Woman*. She currently pastors Relevance in Ghana, West Africa.

To correspond with **Michelle McKinney Hammond** or to book her to speak at your event:

Log on to **www.michellehammond.com**

Follow her on:

    Facebook: **Michelle McKinney Hammond**

    Twitter: **@mckinneyhammond**

    Instagram: **mmh57**

Follow Relevance on:

    Facebook: **Relevance Life**

    Twitter: **@RelevanceLife**

    Instagram: **@RelevanceLife**

    www.relevancelife.org

Other books by Michelle McKinney Hammond

How to Be Found by the Man You've Been Looking For
How to Avoid the 10 Mistakes Single Women Make
The Power of Being a Woman
Sassy, Single, and Satisfied
Sassy, Single, and Satisfied Devotional
Secrets of an Irresistible Woman
Secrets to a Man's Heart
What to Do Until Love Finds You
A Woman's Gotta Do What a Woman's Gotta Do

To learn more about Harvest House books and
to read sample chapters, log on to our website:
www.harvesthousepublishers.com

HARVEST HOUSE PUBLISHERS
EUGENE, OREGON